FOREWORD BY DR. MARGARET FITZGERALD

the Business of
NUR$ING

DR. SCHARMAINE LAWSON

The Business of Nur$ing: The Blueprint

Published by A DrNurse Publishing House New Orleans, Louisiana

A DrNURSE
PUBLISHING HOUSE

Published by
A DrNurse Publishing House
7041 Canal Blvd., New Orleans, La. 70124
www.DrLawsonNP.com

ISBN:
Hardcover: 978-1-945088-40-7
Paperback: 978-1-945088-42-1
ePub: 978-1-945088-41-4

Library of Congress Control Number: 2022930031
This book is printed on acid-free paper.
Printed in the United States of America

Dedication

Dear Skylar Rose, and Wyatt Shane, your ability to love me in spite of my many moods while writing continues to keep me suspended in awe and total adoration of you.

Dear Grandma, I miss you more than life. Thank you for the memories and your abiding spirit, which lives in me. You would be proud of the woman I've become because of your love, rearing, and nurturing. You adopted me at four-months old when you were at the tender age of 60 and somehow always "knew" that I would make something out of myself. I'm so glad you believed in me.

Income Disclaimer

This book contains business strategies, marketing methods and other business advice that, regardless of my own results and experience, may not produce the same results (or any results) for you. I make absolutely no guarantee, expressed or implied, that by following the advice below you will make any money or improve current profits, as there are several factors and variables that come into play regarding any given business.

Primarily, results will depend on the nature of the product or business model, the conditions of the marketplace, the experience of the individual, and situations and elements that are beyond your control.

As with any business endeavor, you assume all risk related to investment and money based on your own discretion and at your own potential expense.

Liability Disclaimer

By reading this book, you assume all risks associated with using the advice given below, with a full understanding that you, solely, are responsible for anything that may occur as a result of putting this information into action in any way, and regardless of your interpretation of the advice.

You further agree that our company cannot be held responsible in any way for the success or failure of your business as a result of the information presented in this book. It is your responsibility to conduct your own due diligence regarding the safe and successful operation of your business if you intend to apply any of our information in any way to your business operations.

Terms of Use

You are given a non-transferable, "personal use" license to this book. You cannot distribute it or share it with other individuals.

Also, there are no resale rights or private label rights granted when purchasing this book. In other words, it's for your own personal use only.

Foreword

It's been a hard, long journey, and now you are about to fulfill your biggest dream — starting your own medical practice. NPs throughout the United States are moving into their own business. You can expand your clinical roles and offer a wide range of innovative clinical services, with the focus mainly on health promotion, chronic and palliative care, accident and illness prevention, clinical specialty practice, support and rehabilitation services, and management consultancy. Efficient clinicians, the nurse practitioners (NPs) are also providing effective and quality services and developing a more positive public image as patient counselors, caregivers, advocates, and educators.

Many of these advanced practice nurses (APNs) seem to have a strong desire to start their own business and become entrepreneurs. Fortunately, there are several ways an NP can strike out on his or her own. However, the two most common problems NPs are facing when making the decision to start their own business are:

1. Lack of proper planning: Opening a medical business is the same as starting any other business. It requires proper preparation and a reasonable time commitment to fulfill all requirements. Keep in mind that nobody else will manage everything for you, so you should plan to follow through on all necessary details.

2. Trying to do it all yourself: You may be a highly skilled clinician, but unless you have managed a business before, you're not competent to do it. You need qualified professionals to help you succeed. Don't try to do everything on your own.

There are no standard solutions when it comes to opening a medical practice. One major element to a thriving practice is getting off to a tremendous start, with the right people, infrastructure, and mechanisms. From securing a business loan, to hiring staff, to selecting software and equipment, a myriad of crucial decisions and important tasks awaits you that may influence your practice operations for the coming months and years. The information given in this book will assist you to start your own medical practice smoothly and professionally.

An important aspect of "The Business of Nur$ing" is that it does not have a typical textbook pattern, so you don't need to start it in the given sequence of chapters, to understand the book. In fact, you can start your journey of "The Business of Nursing" from any chapter, based on your needs and interest.

The book is comprised of five sections. The first section has guidelines about the "The idea", which will show you what it means to be a business owner. Use your personal objectives and goals to decide if entrepreneurship is right for you. The second section is intended to provide an overview of some popular niche skills for NPs. You should go through these business ideas, fine tune them to your own objectives, clinical skills, and the practice rules of your state. The third section is probably the most important part of the book, which is all about the business advisors, licensures, insurances, business forms, and equipment that are required to start a medical practice. It also explains telehealth services and the benefits of remote visits. The fourth section is designed to provide information about different marketing strategies to grow your business i.e., grand opening, social media marketing, online reviews, etc. The final section is a complete checklist for opening a medical practice.

The success of your business will depend on hiring and managing staff members, making realistic budget plans, establishing administrative policies and procedures, monitoring practice expenses, and marketing/promoting the practice. A basic understanding of fundamental business rules will benefit NPs financially and help them develop a competitive advantage in the health care marketplace. This book will help NPs develop a basic understanding of legal requirements, effective business planning, financial management, working with payers, and choosing equipment/electronic health record (EHR) system.

Table of Contents

III. Into the Thick of It

IV. It's Show Time! Getting Started

V. Appendix

I. The Idea!

Opening Your Own Medical Business as an NP: Initial Steps!

From house calls to aesthetic clinics, nurse practitioners are creating a great impact in the field of medicine by opening their own medical practices. Many nurse practitioners with an entrepreneurial spark go for their own practice. Nurse practitioners are proving that the profession is rapidly evolving to bridge the gap between demand and supply of the medical field. No doubt, starting your own business isn't an easy task. However, you can learn from the experiences of others to make your journey a little smoother.

After getting some advanced degrees and certifications, some nurse practitioners make

....

impactful changes in the healthcare business. Currently, choosing an NP profession isn't just about learning nursing skills. In fact, NPs are learning business skills and entrepreneurship to broaden their career choices (Neergard, 2020). By the year 2034, the United States is expected to experience a shortage of more than 124,000 physicians, according to a latest report published by the Association of American Medical Colleges (Boyle, 2021). To fill this huge gap, many of the licensed NPs of the U.S. are starting their own practices.

Always consider the following five points before starting your business:

1. Identify a Niche

The first thing is to find your niche. Determine your target market and ideal clientele before starting a business venture. It is believed that the more niched your service line is, the less competition you will face. Just think that a large number of primary care practices are facing competition against each other because it is not a niche service. On the other hand, there are a few male anti-aging clinics, which are specialized in the management of male pattern baldness.

The most common niche practices among NPs-operated medical businesses are:

- Aesthetics
- Allergy and asthma clinics
- Opioid addiction treatment
- Hormone replacement therapy
- Weight loss clinics
- Stem cell injections

2. Get Social

Select the best social media platform that suits your niche and stick to it. You should become an authority in your niche on that social media platform.

Most healthcare professionals are comfortable using social media to connect with friends and family but are not sure about how to use it in a professional context. The world of social media has wide-ranging implications for healthcare professionals, patients, and public health professionals.

....

Social media can be considered a whole new tool to empower patients. NPs should figure out which social media platforms their target audience uses the most and spend their energy on them. (For example, if you have an idea that most of your patients use Facebook or Instagram, go with those.) Once they get the hang of using those platforms, they may also want some advertising on them as well. This will help them boost their brand's presence and get them in front of the clients/patients they are trying to attract.

Remember that marketing and getting social is the number one function of any kind of business. It does not matter if someone is starting a furniture store or a high-end medical practice, marketing and getting social is the key how to driving clients/patients through the door. Medical practices that do not market properly are doomed to fail. Therefore, it is extremely important that you understand how to market your medical practice. It will certainly make or break your medical practice.

Choosing the Right Social Media Platforms

The real question is which platform is the best fit for your medical practice and how that platform can encourage your business growth. Social media platforms are considered an extremely beneficial healthcare marketing tools used in the medical world. It can be very effective when marketing for NPs and their medical practices. Appropriate use of different social media platforms for NPs can greatly improve their marketing outcomes and drive new patient leads. NPs may have a difficult time using their social media profiles and tracking potential outcomes. However, strong social media marketing plans can help drive new patients, improve patient engagement, share practice updates, advertise healthcare services, expand NPs exposure, improve an NP's credibility as a top healthcare expert, and develop healthy relationships with patients.

Factors such as target demographic, specialty type, geography, and content you create play a crucial role in determining which social media platforms are the best fits to reach your target patients.

....

Facebook

Facebook is considered one of the most successful healthcare marketing tools that should be included in every marketing campaign for NPs. It is a popular social media platform with over 2.9 billion active monthly users as of 2021 (Statista, 2021). When used appropriately, a Facebook page can have great value to a small business.

Facebook can be used to share everything from photos to important updates regarding your practice. You have access to in-depth analytics and advertising tools with a business account. You can use your Facebook page to highlight information like your contact information, working hours, and services you provide.

Facebook is intended to increase brand awareness, patient engagement, and has a great impact on local SEO for a medical practice. Some major advantages of Facebook marketing may include developing brand loyalty, patient engagement and reviews, local SEO, and driving new patients to your practice.

Facebook promotes an incredibly greater level of targeting because of the amount of data they have on their users. This helps you to target paid or organic posts to make sure that your message is delivered to the audience you are looking to attract.

Almost all medical practices and niches are a great fit for Facebook and should use Facebook in their marketing plans.

Instagram

Instagram is one of the fastest-expanding platforms, which is inherently video and image-heavy because users share videos and pictures to connect and engage. It is also an incredibly popular social media platform, with more than 1.1 billion active users in 2021 (Statista, 2021). From Instagram Stories to Instagram Live, there are a number of tools that can be used to promote your products and services on the site.

Instagram for NPs is extremely helpful to engage with patients and share images of lab results, procedures, and other practice updates. Instagram for NPs is an ideal tool for targeting local potential patients, lead generation, any medical retail, and healthcare conferences and events.

Instagram is visual so it can be a better fit for:

- Plastic surgery practices
- Cosmetic procedures
- Orthopedic surgery practices
- Cosmetic Dentistry
- Aesthetic services
- Weight loss clinics
- Physical Therapy
- OB/GYN practices
- Medical spa marketing
- Urology Marketing

Instagram allows sharing healthcare professionals before and after patient results, engaging images and videos of cosmetic procedures, testimonials, and promoting retail products.

Twitter

Twitter is a fantastic social media platform to share original content and lead visitors back to your medical practice website. It has over 600 million active users ranging from 18-29 years of age.

....

Twitter is designed to share information, articles, news, and conversations efficiently and quickly with hashtags used for direct search capabilities. These hashtags help NPs and users find content related to their search. Twitter for NPs can help them to share content and connect with other medical professionals and potential patients.

Almost all medical specialties and niches are a good fit if they are producing consistent and unique content on their website to share.

The following are some common Twitter mistakes that NPs should avoid:

- Lazy posting or direct posting from Facebook.

- Not properly optimized profiles.

- Stagnant profiles.

- Not having an assigned account manager to manage notifications, likes, shares, comments, tweets, and posting in a timely and appropriate manner.

- Just advertising your medical practice.

- Only sharing third-party information.

. . . .

- Not using the platform to engage and connect with other medical professionals in your field.

You can check the following some best nursing accounts on Twitter:

- AllNurses.com
- Patrick McMurray
- Monica McLemore
- Dr. Anna Maria Valdez
- Andrew Lopez, RN
- Nurse Savage

LinkedIn

Many healthcare professionals and business owners are currently using LinkedIn as a digital networking social media platform. It has over 260 million monthly users and is an ideal platform for professional networking (Statista, 2021). It is one of the greatest places to find top talent and promote your business.

LinkedIn is more professional compared to other social media platforms and is geared toward professionals and businesses. Because it is a

....

professional social media platform, it's the ideal place to post job openings and information about your medical practice.

LinkedIn was designed as business development and networking platform for B2B relations. Thus, it is a great way for NPs to directly connect with potential patients and colleagues. LinkedIn is a professional social platform that helps the healthcare community to share articles, medical business news, and promotes positive interactions and professional relationship building.

NPs, hospital systems, and other healthcare professionals can engage and interact by operating LinkedIn as a digital networking social media platform. You can also utilize the platform to search for new hires and quickly review experience, resumes, and recommendations.

Almost all NPs and medical specialties are a good fit for LinkedIn due to the benefits of direct professional networking with potential patients and the healthcare community. However; NPs-owned medical practices benefit more because of the business profile option on LinkedIn. Making a LinkedIn company profile will help to improve your suggested connections and local search rankings.

You can check the following nursing accounts on LinkedIn:

- Bonnie Clipper
- Dan Weberg
- Nicole Thomas
- Renee Thompson - The Workplace Bullying Expert
- Lippincott NursingCenter.com

YouTube

YouTube can be extremely effective for NPs in marketing their practice. YouTube allows NPs and physicians to record and share medical procedures and other relevant content. It is a video-sharing platform where you can upload, view, share, rate, and comment on videos.

Youtube has more than 2 billion active users ranging from all ages. It is the second largest search engine after Google (Statista, 2021). Youtube is a video-based social media platform, which is an amazing option to reach a new and engaging target audience for your medical practice. Youtube is the best social media platform for NPs who want to create and share videos and showcase their particular medical services, testimonials, and much more. Youtube also provides a great search tool and SEO for potential patients searching for specific medical services. It is a lot easier for an NP to come in front of the camera and make a 2-minute video than sit down and write a long-form blog post in his/her busy schedule.

Youtube is an ideal tool for all NPs to share their original content, patient journals, and medical procedures. It takes very little time as compared to constantly writing content.

Pinterest

It is a social media platform designed for only "pins" or image sharing on "boards". This visually oriented social media platform facilitates users to save and show content by "pinning" digital bulletin boards, organized by different categories. For example, an NP might have a health board dedicated to pinning different diseases and their management, another board dedicated to exercise, and so on. Pinterest also has a series of specific types of pins termed Rich Pins, which medical practices can utilize to add particular information to their pins, like service details and location maps. Pinterest is a great option for niche practices.

Images on Pinterest are carefully designed to advertise and promote click through for websites. Pinterest is a great option to share health ideas, DIYs, and more for healthcare professionals and the public to repin and distribute. It is one of the best social media platforms for lead generation, food, health and wellness, and community-related events.

It is noticed that more than 80% of Pinterest's audience is female so healthcare organizations and medical practices looking to appeal to females tend to benefit the most.

- OB-GYN practices
- Senior Care
- Pediatric practices
- Aesthetic practices
- Cosmetic practices
- Plastic surgery services

- Weight loss clinics

- Bariatric

- Dermatology practices

Check the following some best nursing accounts on Pinterest:

- Nurse Nacole

- The Nerdy Nurse

- Mother Nurse Love

- Nurse Jamie

- Scrubs Magazine

- Kati Kleber

Some Best NPs Social Media Accounts You Should Follow

We all use social media on a regular basis. When used professionally, these platforms can be a source of education, connection, entertainment, humor, education, and networking. NPs can use social media platforms for multiple different reasons. Following content generated by NPs on different social media platforms can be a source of staying up-to-date on news and trends in your field. You can follow the below accounts and

....

share them with your coworkers and friends to stay up-to-date on recent industry trends:

From Facebook

The Nurse Practitioner Group: This was created for NPs and NP students to connect and support one another. You can find the support you require within this social community.

The Nurse Practitioner Journal: The major aim of The Nurse Practitioner Journal is to fulfill the needs of NPs by providing them with clinical, practical, and professional information.

Nurse Practitioner Newbies: This is the group for NP graduates and students to ask questions, highlight their concerns, and share pearls of wisdom within this social community.

Nurses Rock: It is a fun and lighthearted page that promotes NPs around the world. You can find inspirational stories and discussions regarding NPs and nursing students.

Funny Nurses: Funny Nurses is a page filled with funny memes and quotes to light up your day. You can find so much here, including hilarity of the nursing profession that could use a little stress relief.

From Instagram

@scrubsmag: You can follow this account for a trusted source for news and lifestyle regarding the medical and health community. It is filled with news headlines and stories you need to know.

@nursingschool: With over 97,100 followers, this account can bring a smile to your face on the toughest workdays – sharing quotes, pictures, and humor to remind you why you select the nursing profession in the first place.

@nursesofinstagram: This account has over 350,000 followers, sharing funny, informative, and inspirational posts for nurses. It also features stylish scrubs for nurses and builds a nursing community to connect and help one another.

Other interesting and informative Instagram accounts for NPs are:

- Nurse Blake
- The Remote Nurse

- The Six Figure Travel Nurse
- Katie Duke
- She's in Scrubs

3. Focus on Consistency

Consistency is the key to your success. With so many tasks to perform and a lot of things to do, an NP entrepreneur may get overwhelmed. You should use online calendars and email list services to prioritize and organize your tasks. Complete your most important tasks first and then move towards other tasks. Using online calendars and email list services will make you consistent in completing your tasks and will prevent your organization from appearing unprofessional.

You can check the following online calendars to prioritize your organizational tasks:

- Google Calendar
- Microsoft Outlook Calendar
- Zoho Calendar
- Cozi Family Organizer

- Jorte
- Apple Calendar
- Calendly
- Todoist
- SavvyCal
- Calendso

4. Advertising

Spread your message to the public about the company's distinctive brand through advertising on different media. As a practice owner, you need to focus on:

1. Offline traditional advertising (Traditional print media and electronic media)

2. Internet online advertising: As patients mostly search for different medical services online, healthcare advertising for NPs and other medical specialties using the internet is on the rise. Thus, online advertising is highly recommended for medical practices.

Online Advertising Options for Medical Practices

Search Advertising

Google Ads is surely the most common online advertising platform. There are different options within Google Ads; however, paid search ads are the most successful options for medical practices. If you advertise with Google ads, your advertisements will appear on the Google Search Network. This means your ads will show up in Google search sites (Google Images, Google Shopping, Google Play, and Google Maps), with search results, and on the Google search partners' websites.

Display Advertising

Display advertising uses audio, videos, and images to promote your medical practice. When advertising with Google ads, these ads will appear on the Google Display Network i.e. Google Finance, Blogger, Gmail, YouTube etc.

Social Media Sponsored Ads

a. *Facebook Ads*

If your practice wants to introduce a new service, procedure, or team member, Facebook advertising is a fairly cost-effective option to boost your reach. These advertisements seem like regular Facebook posts, so people share these ads easily to boost your reach even further.

b. *Instagram Ads*

Like Facebook, Instagram is also a great option to run your sponsored posts to build awareness regarding your services, providers, and practice. If your target patient base tends to be younger, Instagram advertising may be a great way for you.

Video Advertising

Video advertising is an advertisement for your medical practice in the form of a video. Video advertisements come in multiple formats, such as out-stream video (a video that appears by itself), in-stream video (video that appears alongside other marketing material), and interactive (the

....

video plays after a particular activity, such as signing up the newsletter of your medical practice).

5. Enjoy Your Financial and Professional Freedom

Focus on developing a business that reflects your entrepreneurial skills and financial growth.

Should You Start a Business? Your Personal Interests

To start with, you need to find your passion. You really need to figure out if this is something you can do. Starting your practice as an NP takes a lot of time, guts, patience, and dedication. If you don't have these things, it's not worth it for you to take the risk. Obviously, opening, running, and maintaining your own business isn't easy. NPs should understand that they need all the primary things for their own practice that go along with owning any business e.g. bookkeeping, networking, marketing, staffing, social media. You have to work very hard. Therefore, if you like working 9–5 jobs, starting your own business is likely not a good idea.

Nurse practitioners can open their own private practice in many states. But just because you are allowed doesn't mean you should start a business without doing any research and analysis (Wojciechowski, 2021). Ask yourself the following tough, but important, questions:

- What are your primary goals for starting your own practice?

- What will be its location?

- What will be its major focus?

- What will your practice model and payment methods be?

- Will you be able to work long days and nights, weekends, and even holidays for at least a year?

Social media is probably your best friend. You must learn how to use it to be successful in business. Advertisements in local newspapers and electronic media that cater to your community can also be beneficial to your business. Also, getting clients' reviews and high ratings on Google, Yelp, and Facebook may attract new clients.

. . . .

NPs should find a mentor and follow someone who has already established a practice (Kershaw, 2011). A solid 8–10 months of cash on hand is essential while you start your business, build clientele, and start insurance reimbursements. Eventually the "complete autonomy" would be the biggest reward for you in having your own successful practice.

Does Location Matter?

Your practice location will determine how difficult or easy it is for patients to come. Your practice location also determines the practice income. Detailed research of suitable locations is a prerequisite for the choice of your practice location (Chou & lo Sasso, 2009). Always choose your practice location wisely. The location will also have financial and legal implications.

As you evaluate several different places, consider the following four major factors:

1. Legal Requirements

The exact operating rules to open your own practice as an NP may vary depending on the state in which you want to start. Some states require you to start your practice with a collaborating physician, while others allow you to practice independently without a supervising physician. So, if you don't know your state's requirements, your initial step should be to figure this out.

2. Demand of the NP

The U.S. needs more nurse practitioners. According to the U.S. Bureau of Labor Statistics, the demand is especially higher in rural and medically underserved regions.

You should plan to start your practice in these areas so that you can reach the widest scope of patients.

3. Regional Expenses

The costs of operating a business and living differ by region. Variable expenses may include business insurance rates, property rates, utilities, and government licenses and fees.

Remember that payroll also depends on the location of your practice. State minimum wage regulations may also vary from state to state. For example, a receptionist earning minimum wages in Texas will be less than in California.

4. Taxes

As a business owner, you'll have to pay some combination of sales tax, income tax, corporate tax, and property tax. All of these taxes will eventually affect your bottom line. Thus, research the detailed tax environment of the state and city where you want to start your nurse practitioner private practice (Walczak & Cammenga, 2021b). You'll find that certain areas are more business-friendly than others.

As per Tax Foundation, the top five worst tax climate states are:

- Alaska
- Florida
- Wyoming
- South Dakota
- Montana

According to Tax Foundation, the top five business-friendly states are:

- California

- New Jersey

- New York

- Arkansas

- District of Columbia and Connecticut

Does Passion Sell? Feeding Your Passion

While there are multiple different reasons to open your own business, one of the most significant reasons is to focus on working or committing to something that you're extremely passionate about. Starting your own business can certainly improve your income; however, that shouldn't be the primary objective when you go into starting your business. Always focus on starting a business that will facilitate more of the tasks you love to do and less of the activities you don't (de Vore, 2019).

Opting for a business idea for NPs that meshes with your passion will surely make the long days and nights that you'll inevitably work (at least at the beginning, when you start getting things off the ground) easier. You will have to work for long hours, weekends, and even holidays. Your passion will drive you to keep working more and more.

Review the following core issues before your final decision:

1. Ask Yourself if You're Prepared

Opening your own medical practice is the main commitment, as it is with any kind of new business. Taking time to research the uncertainties and implications of running your own business is extremely crucial before making a final decision.

2. Motivations

Check your personal motivations and goals for wanting to work for yourself. The major reasons are your passion, higher income, and a better lifestyle. You should be realistic about the challenges of operating your own business, instead of being overly optimistic.

3. Acquisition of New Skills

You're qualified as a nurse practitioner, but are you qualified to operate your own business? You will need to develop some new skills to manage the financial aspects of your own business, e.g. human resource management, cash flow, budgeting, and business planning. While you don't need to become an expert in all these fields, you should know the basic things about how to work with experts: bookkeepers, accountants, attorneys.

In addition to assessing your weaknesses and strengths, it's important to define and set your business goals. For some individuals, the primary goal is the freedom to work for what and when they want, without anyone ordering them otherwise. For others, the major goal is their financial security. Defining and establishing goals is an important part of choosing the business. After all, if your business fails to meet your established goals, you probably won't be motivated, and it will become difficult for you to wake up each morning and try extraordinary things to make the business successful. Sooner or later, you'll stop putting in the effort required to make the concept work.

. . . .

II. Some Popular Niche Skills for NPs

Some Popular Medical Practices for NPs: Determine Your Niche Practice

It is extremely important that you find a niche for opening your medical business. You need to find a niche that is in demand for your target individuals. You can start your medical practice as a side business and then convert it into a full-time business. This should be the kind of niched service you look into! Opening a business that needs your full-time attention is a recipe for financial tension, stress, and possible failure. The primary goal should be to develop a life of more financial independence and freedom when you start a business. This can be possible with multiple niched side businesses.

More than 20 states in the U.S. now provide full-practice authority (FPA) to NPs (Juda, 2021). The idea of starting your own private medical practice may have crossed your mind if you reside and work in one of these states.

NPs can start their own private medical practice in the following clinical areas:

- Opioid addiction treatment clinic
- Medical spa and aesthetics
- Medical weight loss clinic
- Women's health and HRT (hormone replacement therapy) clinic
- Allergy clinic
- IV hydration clinic
- Dermatology and skincare clinic
- Stem cell and regenerative medicine clinic
- Telemedicine clinic
- Medical cannabis practice
- Ketamine therapy clinic
- Primary care practice
- House call practice or homecare agency
- Specialized care provider business

- Holistic/alternative healthcare practice

- Diabetes specialty clinic

- HIV/AIDS specialty practice

- Midwifery practice

- Mental health NP private practice

- Drug screening practice for legal documentation, DOT physicals, and pre-employment tests

- Occupational practice: consider a practice for workers' compensation or a corporate practice providing services to warehouses, large stores, and manufacturing firms

- A medical-based facility
  - Hospice
  - Assisted living or long-term care facility
  - Adult family home

- Pain management or palliative practice

- Travel medicine: travel health and vaccines

- Urgent care or walk-in clinic

- Wellness care

- Wound care specialists

- Urology/bladder health practice

. . . .

In more detail, then, the following major niche skills and practice areas are out there for nurse practitioners to master and implement into their medical business:

Opioid Addiction Treatment Clinic

It is a niche practice in which few NPs dare to venture. Patients with opioid addiction are very unreliable and need a lot of "babying." This is a great option for the NP who is passionate about helping fight the opioid epidemic that has affected the U.S. over the past 30 years (American Nurse Today, 2021).

It is estimated that over 2 million individuals in the U.S. have an opioid use disorder and more than 800,000 of those individuals' used heroin in the year 2018 alone. The more shocking fact is that around 40,000–50,000 individuals die every year from an opioid overdose. This is a real epidemic, and NPs can play an important role in the fight against this epidemic.

The opioid addiction treatment market is almost a $3 billion market and is continuously growing. According to statistics from the CDC, the rate of opioid overdose in 2020 tremendously increased during the COVID pandemic. These patients need effective treatment. As an intelligent NP entrepreneur, you can stand in the front line while starting this in-demand and successful practice.

You should focus on the following areas to build an impactful and profitable opioid addiction treatment clinic:

- The risks, legalities, and laws associated with opioid addiction treatment
- The mechanism of action for buprenorphine, naloxone, naltrexone, and opioids in general
- The medications related to medication-assisted treatment (MAT)
- Evaluation of the opioid addict patient
- The details regarding urine drug screens
- Diagnosis of opioid use disorder
- Assessment of withdrawal symptoms

....

- Selection of the appropriate medication for patients

- Procedure for obtaining "X-Waiver" to legally prescribe buprenorphine for the treatment of opioid use disorder

- How to induce and maintain the patient on treatment

- How to manage opioid use disorder in a stepwise fashion

- The need for integration of the psychosocial intervention into the treatment plan

- Doses of the medications related to MAT, including buprenorphine, naltrexone, buprenorphine, and naloxone

- Treatment of opioid withdrawal symptoms

Medical Spa and Aesthetics

The medical spa is a medical facility that provides aesthetic procedures under the care of a licensed healthcare provider. These procedures usually include non-invasive options to rejuvenate your body and skin (Writers, 2021).

After graduation from an NP course, NPs need special training and experience with a plastic surgeon or dermatologist (Sam, 2021). They may then obtain certification from the PSNCB (Plastic Surgical Nursing Certification Board). Courses are also available through the IAPAM (International Association for Physicians in Aesthetic Medicine) and AAAMS (American Association of Aesthetic Medicine and Surgery).

Several entrepreneurial NPs are going the medical spa route, starting practices and catering to different cosmetic procedures. In many states,

NPs can start such businesses independently, taking benefit of the state scope of practice laws (International Association for Physicians in Aesthetic Medicine, 2021b). Guidelines regarding the medical spa and cosmetic procedures often vary state by state. For more details, consult the American MedSpa Association that provides a summary of such state guidelines. Many NPs certified to do Botox injections are earning a handsome income.

Medical Weight Loss Clinic

It is another great option for NPs to provide medical-assisted weight loss management and treatment. A medical weight loss clinic is a great opportunity for NPs who want to support the 70% of American adults who are obese or overweight, so they can get back to living a normal and healthy life. If you want to prevent the plethora of obesity-associated conditions in your patients, while making a very handsome income, consider this business.

Medical weight loss clinics can be profitable powerhouses because individuals are sick of feeling and looking bad. What does this mean for an intelligent NP entrepreneur? A tremendous business opportunity in which you are changing the lives of people while making a great income. A win-win!

Pay special attention to the following areas to build an impactful and profitable medical weight loss clinic:

- The legalities and liabilities of medical weight loss

- Developing a successful weight loss plan

- Multiple different diet plans and protocols

- The science of calories and macro-nutrients (carbohydrates, proteins, fat)

- Obtaining malpractice insurance

- Exercise programs for specific patients

- How to start a medical weight loss practice from scratch

- Building a cash flow practice

- Integration of weight loss management with telemedicine

- Marketing of your medical weight loss practice

Women's Health and HRT (Hormone Replacement Therapy) Clinic

Women between the ages of 40–50 who are in the post-menopausal phases are usually a forgotten patient group. Optimize their overall health and make them feel better, and they will hand over money to you happily. You should know everything from bio-identical hormone replacement therapy to screenings, risk factors and side effects, and thyroid replacement.

Females want to feel better. That's why women's health, especially hormone replacement therapy, has been a very hot topic for years. What does that mean for an enthusiastic NP entrepreneur? It's a high-profit business opportunity while having an impact on women's health.

Women's health and HRT (hormone replacement therapy) clinic is a great option for an intelligent NP entrepreneur who wants to build a more financially independent life by delivering care to female patients. This is also a good opportunity for the NP who wants to start a low expense/high revenue practice that could be done part-time or as a side business.

Allergy Clinic

Learning how to manage asthma and other different types of allergies is not extremely difficult. It generally means identifying what the patient is allergic to and gradually desensitizing his/her body to it with "allergy" shots (Kelman, 2019). It is estimated that most allergy clinics have at least two-month wait times. Thus, what does this mean for an energetic and intelligent NP entrepreneur? It's a tremendous market to jump into, because of its greater demands and good profits.

IV Hydration Clinic

NPs can get certification as intravenous (IV) infusion nurses. IV nurses are experts in the administration of IV fluids and medications. They may use a catheter, an IV line, or a central line (NursePreneurs, 2021).

Non-hospital application of IV hydration is becoming more and more popular. It is used to administer hydration, vitamins, and treatment to enhance energy or improve skin quality. There are various opportunities to start your own business dedicated solely to IV hydration. IV hydration clinics are very hot right now and the demand is continuously increasing. This sector is blowing up as patients are demanding this service and it results in tremendous profits for the practice owner.

Do you know the best part of opening an IV hydration clinic for an NP? You can earn money and not even be present in your clinic. Depending on your state's laws, an LPN or RN can work there while you make the money sitting at home. They just need your standing order. Thus, it is a great opportunity for developing your passive income.

IV hydration clinics have been established all over the U.S. over the past five years as patients love them. People prefer a quick fix for everything from a cough to a fever. We live in an era where people want to get better in no time; therefore, as an enthusiastic NP entrepreneur, you can choose this business.

IV hydration clinics mainly target weekend warriors needing a rapid cure for their hangover, individuals with an acute URI (upper respiratory infection) who want to get better faster, athletes who want to hydrate before a marathon, and people who just want to feel better overall. Almost everyone in our society can benefit from an IV infusion; therefore, IV hydration has turned into such a hot medical business.

Dermatology and Skincare Clinic

Dermatology and cosmetic skincare practice is an in-demand and growing medical business. The dermatology and skincare market is a multi-billion dollar market, which is continuously growing year by year. Additionally, the U.S. population is aging and wanting younger looks more than ever before. Thus, what does this mean for an intelligent and energetic NP entrepreneur? A tremendous business opportunity!

Hundreds of patients need affordable and quality dermatological care. It is estimated that standard dermatology practices have multi-month wait times and patients become more frustrated to continue to live with various dermatological issues that are often symptomatic as well. Eczema, acne, melasma, and several other skin conditions plague the appearance of thousands of people in our society. NPs should step up to the plate and help individuals with their dermatological needs.

You can offer dozens of cosmetic skincare products and services in your practice to enhance your practice's offerings, which will eventually increase your revenue streams. People are constantly looking for compounded topical anti-aging, acne, anti-wrinkle, and moisturizing products. You should also learn how to provide these products through your asynchronous telemedicine services from your practice's website, to build a passive income stream.

If you are looking for a high-demand, high margin, low liability, and comparatively straightforward medical business, consider this opportunity.

Stem Cell and Regenerative Medicine Clinic

This is a great business opportunity for the energetic NP entrepreneur who wants to open a very high revenue/low expense cash business that can be run on a part-time basis. Stem cell and regenerative medicine practices are the hottest and highest revenue practices all over the U.S. for generating a seven-figure income as a part-time business. Patients love the results of stem cell and regenerative injections. Several degenerative conditions and chronic pain can improve greatly even after just a single injection (Chlan et al., 2019). Patients almost always come back and refer their family and friends to you. In addition, it is probably the least complicated side practice to start as there are no other complicated prescriptions, medications, labs, or guidelines to follow. You can start it with very little guidance.

....

It is also the one most profitable business a nurse practitioner can open. You can start this business for less than $7,500. The greatest part of this business is that the monthly expenses are very small and only increase as your patient revenue and volume increase. What does this mean for an intelligent NP entrepreneur? A great business idea with more profits! You literally need to handle just four to five patients a month to generate a six-figure income. And especially if you are skilled in trigger point and intra-articular injections, then injecting placental and umbilical stem cells can be extremely lucrative.

It costs very little to open a stem cell and regenerative medicine practice. The most expensive part of this business is the stem cells themselves, which the patient mostly pays for, even before you order them. If your aim is financial and professional independence, consider this niche practice. Multimillionaires are being made of individuals who are running stem cell and regenerative medicine practices. It is time for enthusiastic NP entrepreneurs to get a piece of the pie now!

....

Telemedicine Clinic

The cheapest and easiest way to start a medical business is doing it through telemedicine. This is a constantly growing market and NPs can be on the front lines using this modern-day technology (Balestra, 2018). Why is telemedicine such a great business opportunity for NPs? One simple answer is its independent practice authority. You can live in one state and practice independently in other states such as Arizona, Washington, Oregon, etc., without needing a supervising physician.

Telemedicine offers unlimited opportunities for NPs. Establishing a telemedicine practice is comparatively easy and cheap, compared to a traditional brick-and-mortar business. The five primary essentials are:

1. Personal computer
2. Cell phone

3. Website

4. Online marketing strategy

5. Electronic Medical Record (EMR)

The major challenge an aspiring NP entrepreneur will have when establishing a telemedicine practice will be the selection of the service niche. This is the most important thing for your success (Whelchel, 2021). Along with the marketing, your service niche is the most vital part of your business. Starting a telemedicine business for your primary care office or for urgent care is probably not the best idea. This is overdone and your chances of success are much less. Think of out-of-the-box ideas, just like the person who recently established the online erectile dysfunction telemedicine clinic. Men usually do not like visiting a doctor's office for their erectile dysfunction issues. That practice is making millions by simply conducting a 10-minute online or phone visit and prescribing a six-month supply of Cialis or Viagra. Thus, think out of the box here!

Medical Cannabis Practice

NPs can make a significant portion of their income through performing medical cannabis evaluations. Consider this if your state allows this. Starting a medical cannabis practice is easy and cheap with little liability.

As researchers are learning more about the endocannabinoid system of the human body, the cannabis and cannabidiol (CBD) oil are becoming more popular in managing various health conditions, including:

- Pain management
- Fibromyalgia
- Cancer

Medical cannabis practice is a great opportunity that an NP can use to start a successful side practice (Klein & Bindler, 2021).

You should consider it if you want to start a high-revenue, low-liability, and low-expense niche side practice.

You should pay special attention to the following aspects for building a successful medical cannabis clinic:

- The legal issues associated with medical cannabis

- Issues regarding medical malpractice

- The mechanism of action of medical cannabis

- How to recommend medical cannabis to patients

- The process of identifying how patients qualify

- How to integrate the philosophy for medical cannabis into your practice.

- How to recommend certain medical cannabis products with their dosages for specific conditions

- The risks, side effects, and benefits of medical cannabis

. . . .

- How to start a cash-only practice for a medical cannabis clinic

- How to market your medical cannabis practice

Ketamine Therapy Clinic

This has been a hot niche practice over the past five years for some good reasons: it provides great relief to patients and is a high-demand medical business! Not only is it an effective and a high-demand treatment option, but it is also a cash and highly profitable business (Garde, 2018).

Ketamine is used to manage mental health conditions and chronic pain. It can be administered through oral, intranasal, and intravenous routes, but the IV infusion component is vital to long-term patient success. Many people are actively searching for this treatment option after a standard medical therapy has failed again and again for them. What does this mean for an intelligent and energetic NP entrepreneur? A great business opportunity with low marketing costs because the patient will seek you out! Once

....

you develop your website and start your practice listing, the phone calls from patients will begin coming in! Thus, it is a great instant revenue generator business once you get started.

Many of you are thinking, "Can NPs be allowed to administer ketamine infusions?" The answer is: YES! You are an NP, and it is within your scope to manage mental health conditions and chronic pain. You are also an RN; thus, you are allowed IV infusion therapies. Dozens of NPs in the U.S. own and run ketamine infusion practices with great success!

You should pay special attention to the following aspects to establish a successful and profitable ketamine therapy practice:

- The legalities, regulations, liabilities, and risks of ketamine therapy
- How this therapy is within the scope of practice for an NP
- The mechanism of action of ketamine
- Patient selection and evaluation for the therapy
- Patient education and infusion preparation

....

- Short- and long-term side effects of therapy

- Dose adjustments of ketamine for both mental health conditions and chronic pain

- Patient monitoring during infusion and treatment

- Use of oral, IM, and intranasal ketamine

- Adjunctive medications that can be used during the infusion

- Charting of the infusion and visits

- Marketing of your ketamine therapy practice

Primary Care Practice

This can take place in several settings including your office, an individual's home, worksite, adult daycare, all kinds of residential facilities, and community centers.

House Call Practice or Homecare Agency

The home health and house call industry are a fast-growing market. As one of the largest generations retires and ages, they need care at their home. According to the CDC, almost 60% of adults have at least one chronic problem and 40% have two or more. NPs can start their own home care agency with a business plan, funding, employer ID number, and a state license.

Specialized Care Provider Business

The specialized care provider business is a great business idea for NPs who have mastered a specialized skillset throughout their career and want to use those skills in starting their own business. It is a great opportunity for enthusiastic NP entrepreneurs, who want financial independence and work in-depth in one specialized area.

The following are some common examples of specialized care provider businesses:

- Fertility consulting
- Childbirth training
- In-home care

- Mindfulness and stress reduction
- Lactation consulting
- Holistic or alternative medicine services

III. Into the Thick of It

Business Advisors for Your Medical Practice

One of the most crucial decisions before starting your business is wisely choosing your business and legal advisors. The following are the major business and legal advisors you'll need to run your business smoothly:

- Certified Public Accountant (CPA)
- Bookkeeper
- Healthcare attorney
- Financial planner
- Business coach
- Insurance agent
- Investment advisor

Your Top 3 Key Players: CPA, Bookkeeper, and Attorney

Accountants and bookkeepers both work in different stages of the financial cycle and play an important role in managing your financial matters. Bookkeepers record your business data and accountants further analyze the recorded data. Attorneys look after you on all licensing, contractual, and regulatory matters.

Bookkeepers

The major responsibility of the bookkeeper is to record as well as organize the business data and financial transactions of your business. This recorded data is usually used to prepare tax documents. Some major tasks of bookkeepers may include:

- Managing accounting systems e.g., historical accounts, general ledgers, etc.

- Processing receipts, invoices, payments, and other financial transactions

- Managing payroll as well as employee records

- Preparing and managing financial statements

- Reconciling accounts and organizing reconciliation reports

- Managing any financial loans or debt repayments

Accountants

While bookkeepers record the business data and financial transactions of your business, the Certified Public Accountant (CPA) analyzes the recorded data, ensures the figures are accurate, prepares as well as interprets business reports, and makes sure that all the compliance requirements are being met.

The major tasks of the CPA may include:

- Preparation and adjustment of entries (recording transactions that were not already recorded in the books)

- Analyzing the operational costs

- Preparing the advanced and detailed financial statements of the business

- Completing tax returns

- Assisting you to understand the impact of your financial decisions

The CPA uses the data delivered by bookkeepers in the ledgers. The CPA also helps business owners with strategic tax planning, financial forecasting, and tax filing.

Healthcare Attorneys

There is multiple different licensing, regulatory, and contractual matters to address before a successful medical business can start to flourish and thrive, and avoid future business disputes, legal complications, and even violations of laws. Your primary concern when opening a medical practice as an NP is protecting your interests. Healthcare attorneys provide you the legal support and deal with all the licensing, insurance, and regulatory matters of your practice.

Licensure

NPs should follow the state regulations for holding a professional license in the state. NPs must be licensed in the state in which they work. Many states require NPs to hold master's degrees. Various states require NPs to have obtained national certification. NPs can practice once they've obtained national board certification.

Where Can NPs Have Their Own Practice?

While you can start your own business as an NP, the exact operating rules may vary from state to state. Some states require you to start your practice with a collaborating physician, while others allow you to practice independently without a supervising physician.

The AANP groups each state by full practice, reduced practice, and restricted practice:

Full Practice States or FPA states

NPs are allowed to practice independently and perform all NP practice elements, such as evaluation and diagnosing patients, medication prescription, and managing treatments. Full practice states are:

Alaska	Arizona	Connecticut	Colorado	Hawaii	Iowa
Idaho	Maine	Minnesota	Maryland	Montana	Nevada
Nebraska	New Mexico	New Hampshire	North Dakota	Oregon	Rhode Island
South Dakota	Vermont	Wyoming	Washington		

Reduced Practice

NPs are reduced to at least one element of the NP practice and must collaborate with other healthcare providers, such as physicians, to provide care for their patients. They are not allowed to render all levels of care independently. These states are:

Alabama	Arkansas	Delaware	Indiana
Illinois	Kentucky	Kansas	Louisiana
Mississippi	New York	New Jersey	Ohio
Pennsylvania	Utah	Wisconsin	West Virginia

Restricted Practice

State laws restrict the ability of NPs to deliver independent patient care and require them to operate under the supervision of their collaborating physicians throughout their careers. In these states, an NP's practice is restricted to working under a collaborating physician. These include:

California	Florida	Georgia	Michigan
Massachusetts	Missouri	North Carolina	Oklahoma
South Carolina	Texas	Tennessee	Virginia

For more details and the latest information, you can visit www.aanp.org/advocacy/state/state-practice-environment

Drug Enforcement Administration Registration

The Drug Enforcement Administration (DEA) regulates the prescription of controlled substances from NPs. For prescription of controlled substances, an NP must obtain a DEA number after registration with the DEA. DEA registration is a way of tracking an NP's prescribing practices regarding controlled substances. The DEA number is also a great option for reducing unauthorized prescribing. If state laws do not permit NPs for prescribing controlled substances, the DEA will not issue DEA numbers to NPs. Check the DEA's website https://www.deadiversion.usdoj.gov/index.html for further details regarding DEA registration.

Laboratory License

For an in-office laboratory, you must obtain a CLIA number after registering and complying with the Clinical Laboratories Improvement Amendments (CLIA). The CLIA stipulates that all in-office laboratories be licensed based on the complexity of the tests they offer. Thus, office laboratories are subjected to comply with the CLIA. In offices where lab tests are limited to blood glucose, fecal occult blood, urine pregnancy tests, and urinalysis (urine dips), practices may get exemption from inspection by applying to the CLIA for a letter of exemption.

Complete the application for CLIA certification (Form CMS-116) that is available on the CMS website and deliver to the local state agency in which the laboratory facility is situated. (Check the current list of state agencies on the CMS website).

You can visit on www.cms.hhs.gov/clia for more details.

National Provider Identification (NPI)

NPI is required for both organization and individual healthcare providers. Both individual healthcare providers (physicians, nurses, and dentists) and provider organizations (hospitals, nursing homes, and group practices) are required to get an NPI number if they conduct electronic transactions.

How to Apply for an NPI (National Provider Identifier)

Applying for an NPI is a simple, free, and 30- to 40-minute process that will save your time and headaches in the future. You can apply by mail, online, or through a designated CMS contractor.

To apply online, please visit the National Plan and Provider Enumeration System (NPPES) website https://nppes.cms.hhs.gov/, go through all the instructions carefully, fill out the questionnaire, and submit your online application. The website also contains **FAQs** (frequently asked questions) and other helpful material.

Do I Need to Apply for an NPI as an Individual or Organization/Group?

Sole Proprietorships

If your plan is to practice as a sole proprietorship, you need to apply as a type I (individual) entity. You must submit your SSN (social security number) instead of EIN (employer identification number) even if you have one to move forward.

Incorporated Practices

Eligible practices and organizations, including S corporations, should apply for an NPI as a Type II (organization) entity. Eligible providers working within an organization or practice, including an S corporation, can also submit their application for an NPI as a Type I (individual) entity. It should be remembered that an S corporation representing just one provider is still eligible for a Type II NPI.

....

Obtain Credentials

Once you set up a legal structure, the further step will be to obtain the credentials that'll permit you to start and run your nurse practitioner private practice. You need, at a minimum, your federal tax ID number and business registration.

Tax ID Number

You must register with the IRS to obtain a federal tax ID number. The number will also be used to pay federal taxes, staff hiring, a bank account opening, and apply for business permits and licenses.

A tax ID number, also known as a Federal Employer Identification Number (FEIN) or EIN (employer identification number), is a special 9-digit number. For more details, you can visit the official website of IRS i.e. https://www.irs.gov/businesses

Business Registration

Also, register your practice as a legal entity with the local or state government where you operate your business. You will have to apply and pay a fee for your business registration.

For complete guidelines regarding business registration, please visit https://www.sba.gov/business-guide/launch-your-business/register-your-business and get further details.

Insurances

General Liability Insurance

Protects your business from claims that are caused by:

- Damage of someone else's property

- Bodily injuries to a patient or visitor visiting your clinic

- Advertising injury, such as copyright infringement

General liability insurance is also known as commercial liability insurance or business liability insurance. Remember, it only covers third-party claims and does not protect you if your employees get hurt or your own property is damaged. It also doesn't protect you against legal actions for mistakes in the professional services you deliver.

Other Important Policies for Healthcare Professionals

Although general liability insurance covers several major risks, it does not provide complete protection. Any damage to your own business property or your employee injuries may occur at your medical practice. Other important insurance policies for your business may include:

Business Owner's Policy

A business owner's policy combines commercial property insurance with general liability insurance, usually at a lower rate than if both policies were purchased separately.

Where to Purchase a BOP?

There are dozens of insurance companies that sell business owners policies (BOP). If you already have property insurance, general liability insurance, or another form of insurance from a specific insurer, it's a great idea to request them if they provide you with a business owner's policy. You will see how much cost you can save by selecting the insurance bundle.

. . . .

If you're newly starting your business or if your insurer doesn't provide a business owner's policy, then it is recommended to consider one of the following A-rated insurance companies to purchase your business owner's policy:

Chubb

It is a highly rated insurance company that offers a business owner's policy in almost all 50 states. Through a Chubb BOP online, you can get a policy online.

Based on your business, Chubb will provide you with multiple options to customize your business owner's policy. At a minimum, a business owner's policy includes a bundle of commercial property insurance, general liability insurance, and business interruption insurance. Financial services, professional services, and technology are three main industries that frequently purchase a business owner's policy from Chubb.

Hiscox

It is an A-rated insurance company and one of the most experienced and reputable insurance providers for businesses that have been around since 1901. Hiscox provides business owners' policies for online quotes and purchases in many states. You can complete a short questionnaire regarding your business's insurance requirements and purchase the policy accordingly.

The Hartford

It is an A+ rated insurance provider that offers a business owner's policy in several states. Hartford's BOP bundles commercial property insurance, general liability insurance, and business interruption insurance. Optionally, it also offers businesses to add on professional liability coverage or data breach coverage to a BOP.

Progressive

Progressive Insurance is an A+ rated insurance provider that offers a business owner's policy at lower costs in several states. Progressive's BOP usually combines commercial property insurance, general liability insurance, and business interruption insurance.

Insureon

It is an insurance marketplace that helps you compare offerings from different insurance providers. Chubb, Hiscox, and The Hartford are basically the partners of Insureon, so Insureon acts as the middleman to compare their offerings and find the best deal.

Cyber Liability Insurance

Cyber liability insurance helps you survive cyberattacks and data breaches. It provides protection from you paying for recovery expenses as well as other relevant expenses.

You can search the following insurance providers to purchase cyber liability insurance for your practice:

- Chubb
- AIG
- XL Group
- Travelers
- AXIS
- Beazley
- CAN

- BCS
- Hiscox
- Liberty Mutual
- HSB

Workers' Compensation Insurance

Workers' compensation insurance is required in almost all states for healthcare businesses, which covers medical fees for work-related injuries and illnesses of employees. Workers' compensation insurance provides coverage for medical bills for your employees if they get sick or injured during their job. This policy is important as it not only protects your employees' finances but also minimizes your liability for work-related injuries and illnesses.

You can search the following insurance providers to purchase worker's compensation insurance for your practice:

- AmTrust
- The Hartford
- Travelers
- Liberty Mutual

- Birkshire Hathaway Guard
- Markel FirstComp
- Employers Insurance
- Accident Fund
- AmeriSafe Insurance

Malpractice Insurance

Also called professional liability insurance, this policy covers legal expenses regarding accusations of negligence or errors. You cannot control everything in your practice as an NP. Everyone in your practice, including you, can make mistakes. Malpractice insurance provides a comfort factor against legal actions for negligence and errors in the professional services you deliver.

Check the following insurers to get malpractice insurance for your practice:

- CoverWallet: It is the best option for comparing online quotes.
- Proliability: It offers one of the best liability coverage of Malpractice Insurance for NPs.

- Berxi: It is a great option for including lawyer service in Malpractice Insurance for NPs.

- M&F: It provides the cheapest quotes for Malpractice Insurance for NPs.

- NSO (Nursing Service Organization): NSO offers the most comprehensive Malpractice Insurance for NPs.

- CAN: CAN is one of the best insurers that offer Malpractice Insurance policy customization for NPs.

....

Effective Patient Handling

Reimbursement Options

Reimbursement for NP services might come from any or all the following five major sources:

1. Government payers: Medicaid and Medicare

2. Private insurers: managed-care organizations (MCOs), health maintenance organizations (HMOs), and indemnity insurers

3. Patients who pay their own bills

4. Grants

5. Contracts

As a practice owner, you should investigate all these sources of reimbursement. For example, some private and government agencies may contract with NPs for health services. A pediatric NP can contract with the county school system to provide immunization services or to conduct school physicals. Several diagnostic and procedural testing can be separately billed for each encounter. As a practice owner, you should look for all these opportunities to improve your practice income.

Practice Expenses: Crunching the Numbers

A considerable amount of patient visits is required to sustain a profitable private practice. Before considering opening a practice, you should know how the numbers crunch in your business. It is estimated that it costs a minimum of $200,000 a year to run a small NP practice, excluding physician compensation. Expenses may include:

- Rent
- Payroll and employee benefits
- Office equipment
- Quarterly federal and state taxes
- Utilities
- Telephone and Internet connection
- Answering service

....

- Hazardous waste disposal
- Payment on a start-up loan
- Professional dues and subscriptions
- Supplies
- The fee to register a lab with state and federal governments
- Attorney fees
- Accounting fees
- Collaborating MD fees if you are *not* in a FPA state
- Business travel (travel to patients' homes, nursing homes, educational seminars, and for continuing education)
- Cleaning
- Application fee for hospital privileges
- Insurance (umbrella policy, general liability, professional liability, workers' compensation, unemployment)
- Cellular telephone
- Marketing and advertising

Patient Flow Management

For patient handling, you should have an established way of setting up appointments, greeting patients, obtaining insurance or other reimbursement information, getting clinical intake information (e.g., history, chief complaint, vital signs, old records), handling provider visits, and managing follow-up as required (Jain, 2021).

Appointments

Two common methods are used for scheduling appointments. Appointments may be scheduled manually through an appointment book from office supply stores. Appointments can also be scheduled electronically for appointment-handling software. The choice of scheduling methods is based on the practice size, patients' needs, and providers' preferences.

Your medical office software should have an appointment toolbar with an option to add a patient, see a calendar, add a patient to the waiting list, or search the calendar for available time slots. Electronic scheduling is a quick method that facilitates searching for available appointment time slots.

....

Solo practitioners or small medical practices might not have enough resources for an advanced EMR system or a full appointment scheduling system. Thus, free appointment scheduling software can be a great option for you to get started if you are not quite ready to pay for an expensive appointment scheduling system.

Remember, many EHRs already include patient scheduling as part of their entire suite of functionality. However, if you want something specifically for medical appointments, here is a list of some commonly used free medical scheduling options:

Picktime

It is a cloud-based appointment scheduling software solution that enables your medical practices to streamline processes regarding appointments scheduling, staff management, meetings, and much more. You can use the platform to share appointment links with a patient, send text reminders and emails, and reschedule medical appointments via a user-friendly drag-and-drop interface. The online calendar in the Picktime allows healthcare providers to book or rebook appointments per availability, manage leaves or holidays using labels, and handle any recurring appointment across multiple locations.

Sagenda

Sagenda is a cloud-based patient appointment scheduling software solution designed for small size medical practices as well other businesses. Your patients can easily schedule appointments through Sagenda appointment booking solutions.

You can use Sagenda to share appointment scheduling links with a patient and send texts or email reminders. The tool can be downloaded and installed onto existing practice websites, so it's a great option if you already have a practice website.

10to8

It is a cloud-based scheduling software solution for a medical practice that is looking for appointment scheduling software. It provides a customized scheduling website where a patient can schedule appointments, pay for services, and access existing scheduled appointments.

Setmore

The customizable online booking page of Setmore makes it simple for you to connect with your patients for free. Your practice can embed the online appointment scheduling functionality into your website or Facebook page.

Payment Intake Information

For each patient, the medical administrative assistant or an intake staff person will need to collect the following information:

- Name of the patient

- Address

- Contact number

- Date of birth

- Social Security number

- Payment method: insurance, credit card, cash

- Insurance company name, contact number, and address

- Copy of insurance card

- Emergency contact name, contact number, and address

....

Clinical Intake Information

Your practice will also need a clinical intake form – history, chief complaint, vital signs, and old records – suited to the patient.

Provider Visits

You must establish a system for patient encounters. Always focus on the following basic area for dealing with patients:

- The provider's working scope (either works multiple rooms or handles one patient at a time)

- Patient receiving methods

- Initial interaction of the patient with the attending provider

- Process for taking care of ordering referrals and laboratory tests after an encounter

- Procedures for the history taking and patient education

Follow-Up

You are also responsible for follow-up and review of lab testing, phone calls to patients for follow-up contact, and phone calls to other providers regarding patient issues. You can also hire a medical administrative assistant or other supportive patient care staff for these tasks. If you must do these tasks, there should be proper time built into your schedule. If another support staff member is hired to do these tasks, there must be an appropriate system for communication between the provider, patient, and support staff member, as well as documentation in medical records.

Will Your Practice Use an EHR, and If So, Which One?

Given the benefits of EHRs (electronic health records), it makes sense for your brand-new practice to start with an EHR. However, to answer the question of which EHR is best, you should begin with articles in clinical trade journals about the top EHRs and do proper personal research before your final selection (Notte & Skolnik, 2010). Also, ask other practice owners and your colleagues about the pros and cons of their EHRs.

EHRs for NPs in the Age of Telemedicine

We saw a breakthrough in Telemedicine amidst the COVID-19 pandemic. It is becoming too difficult for healthcare providers to keep normal patient care going, and the EHR system bundled with Telemedicine is the need of the hour for medical practices. As already discussed, NPs can now practice telemedicine without the physical presence of patients, and assist, diagnose and render a management plan for them. Without the EHR system, this might have been extremely difficult and hectic for you.

Here are a few examples of the top EHRs:

- Epic
- Cerner
- Meditech
- CPSI
- Allscripts
- Medhost
- Athenahealth

Examples of some EHRs for solo or small medical practices are:

....

- ChARM HER
- Insync Healthcare Solutions
- Jane
- Praxis EMR
- RXNT
- TriMed Complete

Different Forms of Businesses

There are the following four major options for the business structure of an NP practice (Sastow, 2016):

1. Sole proprietorship

2. General partnership

3. Limited liability company (LLC)

4. Corporation

1. Sole Proprietorship

In a sole proprietorship, the individual and the businesses are the same. Any legal liability or debts are the sole responsibility of the business owner. The business owner is responsible for filing tax information along with his or her tax return. The deduction of the year-end losses is made from the owner's taxable income. On the other hand, year-end profits are added to the owner's taxed income accordingly. Benefits of a sole proprietorship may include:

- The business owner takes all decisions independently.

- Year-end losses can be deducted from the owner's personal/family income.

- There is no potential liability for the bad judgments, purchases, and mistakes of a partner.

- There is no chance of double taxation as is the case with a corporation.

The major disadvantages of a sole proprietorship are:

- There is no one to support with expenses and maintenance of the business.

- Ups and downs are handled by the owner alone.

2. General Partnership

A general partnership is an unincorporated form of business involving multiple partners. It is a business relationship involving multiple owners or business entities. Most general partnerships make clear the relationships among the owners or parties in a partnership agreement. If there is no pre-defined partnership agreement, state rules govern the relationships. In a general partnership, partners are liable for the legal liabilities and debts of one another. Partners share administration, decision-making, profits, and workload in some manner that is agreeable to all. Losses and profits in a general partnership are equally divided and added or deducted to a person's tax forms.

The general partnership has a tax form that contains the record of the distributions of losses or profits to the individuals involved in the partnership. Legal action against any partner implies liability for all partners. Similarly, a debt incurred by any partner will be shared by all partners.

. . . .

The main decisions to be taken by partners may include:

- What occurs if one individual wants out?

- Who inherits if an individual dies?

- How will losses and profits be divided?

- What contribution to the business expenses will each individual make?

- How will responsibilities be divided?

- How will legal decisions be made?

- How will disputes be settled?

3. Limited Liability Company

An LLC (limited liability company) bundles some of the best elements of a general partnership with the best elements of a corporation. State laws may vary regarding the elements of limited liability companies. However, the general provisions of LLCs may include:

- Total income is passed through to the partners of an LLC, as in a general partnership.

- Losses are passed through to the partners, as in a partnership.

- Partners are liable for the debts of the LLC only up to a certain limit.

- Partners agree on operational mechanisms through a predefined written agreement. If there is no written agreement, disputes are settled and managed according to state law related to LLCs.

The major advantage of an LLC is that it bundles the best of partnerships and corporations.

There are also some disadvantages, such as:

- A state may not own the LLC in this legal type of business entity.

- The regulatory laws are not as extensive in addressing LLCs as they are with the other forms.

- States may have some complex pre-requisites that must be met prior to forming an LLC.

....

- An individual member in an LLC is not individually liable for lawsuits from the actions of another partner.

All members of an LLC have usually agreed on operational mechanisms through a predefined written agreement. Ideally, each member should be represented by his/her own attorney when negotiating these agreements. Year-end losses and income are passed on to the individual members, typically based on the percentage of their ownership. The tax return is filed by the LLC to report the amounts passed through to the members.

4. Corporation

A business entity with its own specific identity. Although one individual may be the sole stockholder, officer, director – the owner – the corporation will always be considered a separate legal entity. The corporation owns its specific identifying number with the IRS (Internal Revenue Service) and files a tax return. Decisions are taken by a board of directors, officers, and stockholders.

....

The major advantages of a corporation may include:

- When several members have an ownership interest in the business, there are certain established mechanisms for dispute resolution and decision making.

- There are standard mechanisms for dividing losses and profits, depending on the capital contribution and professional work performed.

- The business expenses are taken from a central pool prior to the distribution of profits to stockholders.

- There are certain legal limits on the personal liability of members.

The main disadvantages of this business form are:

- A great deal of paperwork is needed by federal and state governments.

- Corporate profits are taxed; thus a partner could pay tax once on corporate profits and again on a profit distribution.

Corporations can be distributed as S- or C- corporations.

. . . .

C-Corporation

A C-corporation files income tax returns at the corporate level. It will seldom have a notable taxable income because salaries paid to the staff are tax-deductible expenses. All medical expenses are completely deductible in a C-corporation and there are greater deductions available for retirement plans.

S-Corporation

Structured as a small corporation that meets some specific IRS (Internal Revenue Code) requirements. S-corporations may pass income (along with other deductions, losses, and credits) directly to shareholders, without paying federal corporate taxes. There are solid restrictions on the types of shareholders (not more than 35 shareholders are allowed). As with sole proprietorships and general partnerships, there is limited deductibility for retirement plans and medical expenses.

The Key to Success: Hiring the Right Staff

The question of hiring the right staff is always on the mind of the new entrepreneur. It is believed that hiring even one employee can change everything. Your staff can make or break your business. Staff hiring is critical to the success of your medical practice. An early decision to be taken is the essential number of your support staff. What type of talents and skills do you require to run your business? Where can you find these employees?

As an NP, the minimum services you need to run your practice may include:

- Reception/appointment making
- Billing

- Cleaning
- Accounting
- Payroll
- Legal
- Medical assistance

Remember, you can get most of these services on an as-needed basis as opposed to hiring employees. For example, medical billing is usually done by billing services, as is payroll. Appointment making and reception services, however, are always done by employees of your practice.

Determining Staffing Needs

Your NP private practice will require several employees. You'll need nurses, a receptionist, a phlebotomist, an accountant, and an office manager. You may also consider hiring additional nurse practitioners, a sonographer, medical assistants, or care coordinators.

For each job position, you should write a short job description along with the standard market salary and benefits package. It'll also be beneficial to develop an organizational chart, which demonstrates the reporting relationships among employees.

Business Planning

The success of your business is closely related to multiple factors that can be researched before opening the business. These factors may include:

- The need for your services in the community

- The interest of the community in your provided services

- The size of the patient pool in the community

- The willingness and mindset of the community to use your services as an NP

- The options of reimbursement for third-party payers to NPs for services

The best option to plan for a successful NP practice is to develop a business plan. A business plan for an NP practice must include the following basic items:

- A detailed list of services delivered to patients
- Proof of the need for those services
- An overview of the practice's income compared with its expenses
- A short description of the stakeholders who are opening the business, including their relevant skills and experience
- A comprehensive organizational plan
- A plan for managing the routine activities
- Potential problems and possible risks
- Investment needs

Getting a Business Loan

As a practice owner, you may need a venture capitalist's investment or a bank loan to cover the expenses of your start-up. A concise and comprehensive business plan will set out the complete costs of your start-up along with the plan for repayment. A successful business plan highlights the potential adversities and weak areas of your practice, providing you an opportunity to respond before there is a failure.

The major resources for detailed information on business plans are the Service Corps of Retired Executives and the Small Business Administration. Please visit their websites https://www.score.org/ and https://www.sba.gov/ for more information. Other useful resources are business-oriented community groups, business consultants, web articles, professional organizations and journals, and public libraries.

Take a Look at the Big Picture

An NP planning to open a medical practice should take a look at the healthcare industry in general, and especially the environment in the NP's geographic area. Whether there is a demand for the NP in practice to fill, whether there will be good business support to grow the practice, and whether there are any other legal issues to manage are three major areas that an assessment of "the big picture" can cover. The big picture for a medical practice will include the business environment, laws regarding NPs, the competition, and public and patient perceptions about NPs. All of these factors will determine how your practice will perform and whether it will survive or not. A lender or an investor reviewing your business plan will be inspired by a plan that considers the big picture into account.

Take a Look at the Smaller Picture

An NP planning to start a medical practice should also consider how business ownership and entrepreneurship will affect her/his life. Possible effects of entrepreneurship and small business ownership on an individual's life may include:

- Difficult to separate the work life from the personal life.

- Need of time and money investment in start-up.

- Inconsistent and irregular income while the practice is growing.

- Ambiguity regarding the success of the business.

- Concerns about the ability of coworkers or partners to hold up their end.

Doing Medical Business

Various responsibilities come with being a business owner, such as:

....

- Securing the confidentiality and privacy of patient records.

- Accomplishing the responsibilities of an employer.

- Registering your practice name with the local government as per rules and regulations.

- Disposal of hazardous wastes as per recommended guidelines.

- Complying with building codes and fire marshal inspections.

- Maintaining the lab facilities as per state and federal laws.

- Ensuring that firing and hiring are done according to the non-discrimination provisions of law.

- Ensuring the provision of malpractice coverage for the company or providers.

- Obtaining general liability for your medical practice.

- Providing after-hours coverage and contact information

Beyond the Traditional Brick and Mortar Practice: The Telemedicine Model of Practice

The current COVID-19 pandemic has greatly influenced how providers bestow healthcare services to the patients they serve. Before the pandemic, the use of telemedicine was very limited due to reimbursement and regulatory barriers (Rutledge & Gustin, 2021).

Amidst the pandemic, commercial and federal payers temporarily relaxed telemedicine restrictions and provided extra funding to expand telehealth services. It is believed that NPs who mainly depend on in-person patient visits can use telehealth services to continue rendering care while adhering to the compliance regulations. Telemedicine has overall become the most essential tool for delivering primary care services.

Telemedicine is the use of electronic communications and information technology to deliver remote medical services to patients. The digital transmission of remote clinical diagnosis and assessments, clinical imaging, and video consultations with consultants are some examples of telemedicine services.

Telemedicine services use modern technology to deliver a broad range of health services from NPs and other wider range of providers. Telehealth services may include:

- Awareness sessions for patients and their families about a diagnosis or management

- Review of surgical or diagnostic results

- Nutrition counseling for healthy weight management

- Mental health counseling for depression, anxiety, or other psychological issues

Remote Telemedicine Nursing

The current COVID-19 pandemic has accelerated the adoption of remote telemedicine nursing, with more patients willing to receive virtual care. In essence, remote telemedicine nursing is the use of technology to provide health education and to support clinical healthcare and healthcare administration in remote areas.

Remote telemedicine nurses rely on multiple different modes of communication and information technology to evaluate, treat, and manage different health conditions. NPs use telecommunication technology such as email, telephone, video conferencing tools, online patient portals, web cameras, personal health applications, VOIPs, store and forward sharing methods, and instant messaging services to provide high-quality care to patients remotely. This can make a huge difference between life and death for those who need prompt care but do not have access to healthcare providers.

NPs can conduct remote sessions from their homes, outpatient care facilities, crisis hotlines, trauma centers, healthcare facilities,

....

physician clinics, or anywhere where appropriate technology is present. Remote telemedicine nurses can get a patient's glucose readings and blood pressure, evaluate the patient's oxygen saturation, respiration, and heart rate, or even guide patients on how best to manage a burn and dress a wound.

Equipment for Your Medical Practice

Practice Management Systems

The major key to choosing the right practice management system for your NP practice is making sure that it meets the specific requirements of your practice – "one size fits all" does not apply here. You must thoroughly research and choose your system carefully to avoid any inconvenience. The practice management system is usually a high-cost purchase, so pay special focus to your projected requirements; if you purchase a system that does not have certain modules that your practice may require in the next three years, you may end up having to convert all your data to a new system, which will be extremely time-consuming, and disruptive to practice operations.

....

Staff Training

The purchase price of your practice management system should include training specific to the system. Ideally, the training should include system set-up and customization, reports, day-to-day functions (from patient scheduling to billing), and electronic medical records.

Purchase Options

You can purchase or lease practice management systems. For taking advantage of several tax benefits, consult your CPA before taking the final decision to purchase or lease.

Telephone Systems

Purchase telephone software and hardware only after determining the following requirements of the practice:

- Total number of voice and data lines
- Number and form of telephone sets (e.g., cordless, display, non-display)
- Availability of the voice mail option, with or without outgoing messaging

- Music-on-hold or messaging capabilities

- Remote programming for forwarding of the call

Because the requirements of a practice may change over time, the phone system should have some expansion potential in terms of the number of voice and data lines, the number of sets, and system characteristics. Maintenance agreements from the vendor or manufacturer should be available beyond the original purchase.

Medical Supplies and Equipment

There are several sources of medical supplies and equipment for your practice. You can buy them directly from companies, or through websites, mail order catalogs, or sales representatives. Always monitor the price and quality of these medical supplies. When purchasing medical supplies and equipment, consider the following requirements:

- Your practice size

- Security

- Ease of use

- Appointment tracking
- Patient scheduling
- Appointment tracking
- Physician scheduling
- Patient information
- Demographic information
- Billing
- Collections
- Office routine
- Receipts
- Practice performance measures
- Managed care requirements

Physician Collaboration

Providing optimal care is the major focus for all healthcare providers, regardless of title. However, if the state requires a physician collaboration agreement for NPs, then how do you handle it? If state laws require a collaborative agreement for your NP practice, you will need a collaborator before starting your practice (Brunner, 2019).

The first step is to determine what the state law needs in the way of this agreement. Is it a signed written agreement to consult when required, or is it more engaged, such as signatures on prescriptions and charts, a quarterly review of charts, and monthly meetings?

The next step is to create a list of possible collaborators. NPs will prefer a collaborator who has a similar philosophy of patient care, will be competent, will be easily accessible when required, and will do what is required for a reasonable price.

The third step is to understand and discuss the NP's requirements, the state's laws, and fees with the potential collaborator. Many collaborators are concerned about increasing their liability for malpractice lawsuits if they collaborate with an NP. Thus, malpractice insurers may discuss all these concerns and liability issues with your potential collaborators. If a physician's premiums increase, then that cost will be the responsibility of the NP.

The next step is to measure the potential expenses and contributions of various possible collaborators. The fifth and final step is to draft a professional services agreement between the NP and the physician collaborator, according to protocols or guidelines, required by law.

Of course, multiple factors determine the levels of success of this collaboration. Finding the best match between the physician collaborator and an NP is mainly based on the specialties, competencies, and skills of both. In addition, both parties will realize that their ability to communicate effectively and trust each other is a major determinant in achieving the desired goals.

Different Types of Practice Models

Cash-Only Practice

In a cash-only practice, you can charge what you think your service is worth. You are not required to battle with insurance companies for reimbursements, nor does your payment model change according to the desires of insurance companies. The primary challenge of a cash-only practice model is marketing and defining your target demographic.

Concierge

There are multiple forms of concierge practice model, but the traditional and the most common form is where the patient pays an annual or a monthly fee that provides them direct and continuous 24/7 access to the practice. The practice profits not only from this monthly or annual fee but can also bill insurance companies for patient visits.

Direct Primary Care

With this specific model, providers do not take any insurance, but rather depend entirely on the monthly/annual fee from patients. All labs and visits are paid for by the patient.

Hybrid Practice Model

A combination of the traditional practice and the concierge model.

House Call Practice

This specific practice model does not essentially require a physical office. Based on the NP's concern about billing overhead, the house call practice may or may not participate with insurance plans.

Traditional Insurance Practice

This practice is the single most common and expensive model going. Not only are insurance plans reducing the prices they'll pay NPs, but their requirements are also constantly increasing regarding the practice, such as pre-authorizations, EMR requirements, etc. The traditional insurance practice is still the most viable option with optimum patient care.

Telemedicine Practice

The current COVID-19 pandemic has greatly increased the adoption of remote telemedicine nursing, with more patients willing to receive virtual care. In the Telemedicine practice model, NPs use the technology to provide health education and to support clinical healthcare and healthcare administration in remote areas. They rely on multiple different modes of communication and information technology to evaluate, treat, and provide high-quality care to patients remotely.

Virtual Group Practice Model

A virtual group is defined as a bundle of two or more TINs (tax identification numbers) composed of solo providers and/or groups of up to 10 eligible providers who select to ally themselves for contributing and reporting under the MIPS program.

IV. It's Show Time! Getting Started

It's Show Time

Grand Opening

You must be excited about starting your new business. You have to create some excitement for others too, and a grand opening celebration is one of the best options for doing this. From beginning to finish, your events must scream, "We're going to start. We're going to operate. We're ready. We're different from our competitors. We want to inform you and want you to do business to join us."

Undoubtedly, you have planned every aspect of your new practice for months. You've:

- Selected the perfect name for your practice

- Developed a strong referring network

- Carefully planned your practice design

- Evaluated your marketing plans to ensure you have properly identified your potential customers and patients, and how you will approach them

Here are some ideas for making the most of your medical practice's grand opening:

1. Do Some Special Things for your Community

You can plan first aid sessions, free blood sugar or blood pressure screenings, and bone marrow donor registration. Adding these special things for the community to your grand opening can help attract the public to your event.

2. Include Local Leaders

Politicians usually like a good old-fashioned ribbon cutting event, particularly the event that is focused on providing quality health care to their constituents. Contact your local city mayor, council member, senator, or other political leaders to see if they want to be the special guests at your event. Offer them a platform to deliver a short speech along with the ribbon cutting ceremony.

3. Invite the Media

Once you have included some special things for the community and your local leader scheduled to attend, it will be great to invite reporters and media personnel. Reach out to local TV reporters, newspaper writers, and radio channels to see if they want to cover your medical practice's grand opening event.

Remember to use social media platforms to promote your event and turn the visitors into your loyal patients. Your practice's Instagram or Facebook page is a great source for the event details, photos, services, and special offers.

Marketing Plan for Your Business

How Can You Get Patients to Come to Your Practice?

An NP who opens a new practice will need to attract new patients along with patients with whom the NP has already established a relationship. There are costs involved for both options (Gandolf, 2020). Whether you are looking for new or old patients, proper marketing efforts are always essential.

Marketing involves flyers, letters, ads, speaking engagements, TV appearances, radio announcements or talk shows, web pages, social media, or newspaper articles. Through appropriate marketing strategies, potential patients know about your services and the benefits of visiting.

Some basic principles of marketing may include:

- The marketing message should be repeated multiple times before an individual learns it.

- Develop a feeling of affiliation with the practice.

- Develop an image or logo for your practice along with the marketing message.

- Think and work to exceed the patients' expectations. Your patients not only will attach to your practice but also will recommend it to others.

Understand Your Competitors and Market

Great marketing plans involve long-term investments supported by a strong commitment and a proper budget to resume the plan, even though outcomes often are not too fast. You must understand your target population before marketing. You should identify the main competitors of your practice, your referrals, and insurance companies in the area.

The major characteristics of marketing are:

1. **Community demographics:** Pay special focus to population growth rates, gender distribution, and age.

2. **Local healthcare services:** Quality and quantity of NP practices, hospitals, and other healthcare facilities in your area.

3. **Referrals:** The process of developing referrals is all about building relationships. To create new referrals, develop a continuous communications program to make sure it is working constantly. The purpose of any communications program is to educate provider referral sources regarding how you can support them. Your marketing plan should have the potential to communicate with your potential customers and patients on various platforms.

4. **Website design:** A supportive website design means your website should support and respond to a user's behavior and his/her device environment that includes screen

size, platform, and orientation (such as smartphone, laptop, and iPad). In simple words, your website design should have the full potential to adjust according to the user's priorities. Your website should be simple and easy to navigate, even on short screens.

5. **Social media:** Twitter, Facebook, and LinkedIn are some examples of social media platforms that can be used to market your practice. You should understand how to use social media for your NP practice.

6. **Email:** Improve your brand through a content-rich email marketing program on an ongoing basis. It informs and makes your potential customers and patients aware of the services you provide and the benefits you offer.

7. **Paid advertising:** There are various paid advertising tools like LinkedIn Ads, Facebook Local Awareness Ads, and Google AdWords that bring more patients, referrals, and recognition.

8. **Postcards and brochures:** Today's customer is bombarded with extremely heavy digital marketing content. Postcards and brochures

can be used as a unique marketing tool, which can easily catch the attention of your potential customers and patients through their friendly, attention-grabbing content.

9. **Internal marketing:** Marketing your business actually starts the minute a patient walks in the door. The office signage and décor, the policies of the practice, and the attitude of the staff members must create a professional impression on your patients, as well as referring physicians.

Some Popular Niches for NPs

As an NP, you can start your business relating to your interest, skills, passion, and certifications. The key is in identifying the need and converting problems into opportunities (Duquesne University, 2020). There are numerous opportunities for NPs to become an entrepreneur if they are innovative and competitive. Whether searching for home-based businesses for NPs or traveling to different patients, there are endless business opportunities in line with your schedule, interests, and skills. These opportunities can be categorized into four major groups:

1. Clinical practice opportunities

2. Consulting business opportunities

3. Retail opportunities

4. Educational business ideas

1. Clinical Practice Business Opportunities

- Primary care practice in worksites, homes, and multiple other settings

- Delivering primary, occupational, and wellness care for corporate practice

- HIV/AIDS specialty care clinics

- Diabetes specialty care clinics

- Aesthetics and medical spa practice

- House call practice

- Alternative/holistic healthcare practice

- Mental health private NP practice

- Medical-based facilities like assisted living facilities, adult family homes, hospices, and continuing care facilities

- Pain management practice

- Walk-in/urgent care clinic

- Wound care clinics

- Bladder health clinics

- Midwifery practice

- Men's/women's healthcare practice

- Travel health medicine and vaccines
- Occupational practice to provide workers' compensation
- Drug screening clinics for pre-employment tests, legal documentation, and DOT physicals
- Mobile medical practice
- Surgical centers (with the support of other healthcare professionals like CRNAs)

2. Consulting Business Opportunities

- Exercise/fitness consultancy services
- Case management services for life planning, geriatrics, or estate planning
- Senior consultant for nursing homes or assisted living facilities
- Bioterrorism consultancy services for government agencies and healthcare businesses
- Legal nursing consultancy services
- Occupational health consultancy services

- Infotainment consultant (for TV shows, plays, radio, etc.)

- Disaster preparation and management consultancy for different agencies

- Health coach for wellness care, menopause, and lifestyle modifications

- Day-care consultancy services for specialty populations

- Corporate health consultancy services

- Infection control consultancy services

- Patient care navigation consultancy

3. Retail Opportunities

- Wellness spa (offering skincare treatments)

- Retail health clinic

- Health food retail store

- Fitness facility

- Nutritional supplements and herbs business (selling online or in-store)

4. Educational Business Ideas

- Nursing education (teaching other nurses who are continuing with their education)

- Delivering preparation courses for certification and licensing exams

- Training NPs specialty procedures, ACLS, AED, EKGs, and BLS

- Public health awareness programs, such as CPR or childbirth

Choosing the Best NP Entrepreneur Idea

There are several kinds of business for NPs. However, you should completely evaluate which type of business is best for you before investing your money as well as time.

For this, you should think about the following:

Your Skills

Ask yourself the following questions to get an insight into what you're good at.

- What aspects of the current healthcare system do I enjoy the most?

. . . .

- What aspects of the current healthcare system do I like the least?

- Do I like sales?

- Is there a specific patient population that I prefer and like to work with?

- Would I enjoy tasks that dealt more with administrative activities and less with people?

- Can I find good solutions to existing problems?

- What are my weaknesses at my current job?

Your Schedule

Will you want to work on your business full-time or part-time? You can take your start from a part-time business. Taking your start with a side business and then developing it into a full-time practice helps you:

- Determine the sustainable demand for your practice, products, and services

- Work through any workflow or operational problems before diving in

....

If you decide to go with a full-time business, research thoroughly to determine:

- The required amount of start-up capital
- Your target market
- The possible risks
- The expected outcomes

Feeding Your Passion

Doing things that you're passionate about is vital. You should focus on your favorite to-dos before starting your own business. However, you should also mesh your passion with your skills and profitability, in order to achieve your desired outcome. Always look for the needs of your target market and potential clientele before starting.

Strategies for Success

- Evaluating your skills and readiness
- Learning the basic rules of running a business, such as legal aspects, business planning, and federal/state regulations
- Market research and analysis
- Marketing your business

- Consulting experts, such as healthcare attorneys, accountants, and billing and coding experts).

- Making future plans

- Re-evaluating the feasibility of your business plan

Social Media Marketing

Just like every modern business, NPs should also follow a tried-and-tested digital marketing strategy to promote their business. Digital marketing is usually built around social media, analytics, ads, and more. You can use different approaches for digital marketing, depending on multiple factors like your location, budget, industry, and potential customers and patients.

Social media is an extremely beneficial tool in almost all kinds of businesses, including a medical practice. Indeed, since a medical practice caters to the public and healthcare providers are considered guardians of our health, it's logical to engage and communicate with patients on their preferred social media platforms (Phillips, 2015).

You can use different social media platforms to pose questions to your potential patients, publicize interesting health or nutrition literature, dispense your opinions along with blog posts, and make awareness campaigns for the health and wellbeing of people.

Many healthcare providers have significantly boosted their practice via social media platforms, such as Facebook, Twitter, Instagram, YouTube, and Pinterest. You can talk about public health issues, health awareness topics, nutrition, and food and fitness. In this way, you can use the digital marketing approach to promote your own practice.

As for which social media platforms are suitable for medical businesses, this mainly relies on the type of content you wish to post. All the major social media platforms will help you interact with your potential patients. You can assess their preferences and formulate a strong digital marketing plan.

Facebook is considered the most popular social media platform for promoting a medical practice. However, you cannot ignore Instagram, Twitter, YouTube, and Pinterest. Additionally, you can show your online presence by participating in ongoing conversations on relevant Facebook, Twitter, and LinkedIn groups. Websites like Quora are also a great option, where you can help patients solve their health issues and drive more traffic to your own website.

Posting on Social Media

Perhaps, when you commence, you are going to be posting most of the content yourself. However, sooner or later you may need some assistance due to your busy schedule. This is something you can find and pass on to the right assistant.

You can use different social media analytics tools to schedule your social media posts so that you can focus on other important things. Check out Hootsuite and Buffer. Both of these are free and quite helpful (you can upgrade to paid version for more advanced services and functionalities).

Researching and Planning

It may be funny, but sometimes what we think our clients and patients need from us and what they actually need from us can be poles apart.

Do some research and listen to what your clients and patients are asking you. What are their main fears and challenges? Remember, always monitor your social media analytics to both help create more engaging content and to watch out for trends your practice should follow.

Advertising: Free or Paid?

Most of NPs start using Facebook or other social media platforms to just share their content (sayings, photos, personal posts, health updates, and pertinent news) with their followers and friends.

However, for maximum reach, you need to get involved with "boosting" your posts on different social media platforms. In simple words, you'll have to pay to reach a new target audience. Remember, social media advertising is still the most cost-effective option as compared to search engine PPC (pay-per-click).

Now it's Your Turn!

It is highly recommended that you should look closely at the content you plan to post to social media. Make sure it meets your standards for both the quality as well as privacy of the data you are sharing.

Online Reviews

Reputation management is necessary for any business, but especially for the medical business. Patients have become savvier than ever, analyzing reviews before visiting a restaurant or purchasing a product, so why wouldn't they do the same before selecting a medical practice for their personal health?

It is recommended that you should include a patient review platform on your website and encourage your patients to leave reviews describing their experience. You may also ask them to share reviews on their own private social media platforms (American Association of Nurse Practitioners, 2019).

Online reviews, in the modern digital world, can make or break your medical practice. Today, it has become easier than ever to share and post reviews online about a medical practice. By putting some effort into this domain, you will develop a wide pool of positive reviews that will neutralize some negative comments from unhappy patients. For posting online reviews, you need to create your online listing on:

- Google
- Bing
- Facebook
- Yelp
- Foursquare

Reviews May Create an Initial First Impression

If your medical business has review after review showering your staff and providers with praise and positive feedback, this keeps you in a great position to convert these reviews into a returning patient. Take the tremendous reviews and highlight them by placing them on your website. Refresh them regularly for new reviews on your website for patients to read as they search your services.

Make Improvements with Patient Feedback

A good medical practice will take patient reviews seriously and use them to improve their services. Are there reviews about how not-so-comfortable your chairs are? Perhaps it is time for some new chairs for the waiting room. Are there reviews about the hygiene of the bathroom? Maybe you should hire a new weekly cleaning crew. A good practice owner will investigate all reviews and take the necessary steps to improve the customer experience.

Respond to Reviews to Show Your Practice Takes Feedback Seriously

For a potential patient searching for your services, it can be really disappointing to see no response from the owner for a series of negative and positive reviews. Without a response, it is difficult for someone to guess if any reviews are being seen. If someone takes the time to leave you a comment, you should consider responding to them. Even your simple "thank you" will be an indication that you have seen the review. Try to respond to as many reviews as you can, as soon as possible.

V. Appendix

Checklist for Opening a Medical Practice

This checklist will provide NPs with a comprehensive description of things to do, decide upon, and think about before establishing a business. Some of the options may vary from state to state; however, most of them are common to NPs in all states.

Administration

A practice may have a single owner, or it may have multiple owners. The three primary business structures are sole practitioner, partnership, and corporation. If an NP is establishing a practice alone, he/she will be responsible for making administrative decisions. However, when more than one owner is involved, there are some established guidelines for decision-making that are essential for running a practice.

Billing

You can hire a billing clerk. However, many practices hire outside companies (third-party) to perform their billing tasks, which usually charges a fixed fee per bill or takes a small percentage of the income.

Business Associates

Under the HIPAA (Health Insurance Portability and Accountability Act), business associates are bound to protect the security and privacy of the PHI (patient health information) if a business associate has access to this sensitive information. Therefore, your practice must have a contract or proper agreement with business associates to this effect.

Business Form

A sole practitioner is responsible alone for the business. All legal and tax liabilities lie with the sole practitioner. In a partnership, all partners share the liabilities as well as the profits. Each partner is responsible to pay taxes on his/her own earnings. There are multiple different forms of corporations. The employees in a corporation pay taxes on their income, the corporation itself pays taxes on profits, and the stakeholders pay taxes on their dividends. A corporation that provides clinical services is generally required by state regulations to be a pertinent form of the corporation: a PC (professional corporation) or PA (professional association). An LLC (limited liability company) is basically a combination of some features of the corporation and some features of a partnership. An LLC should be considered when a practice has multiple providers who are considering a partnership. An NP should consult an attorney when selecting a business form.

Call

Establish a communication system to make sure that patients have 24-hour access to providers.

Chaperones

The requirements for a chaperone during a patient encounter are based on the nature of the encounter as well as the gender of the patient and the provider. You should consider the need for chaperones while staffing.

Compliance

If your organization is going to bill third-party payers, you should establish a compliance plan to demonstrate how you will oversee the billing according to payer rules. For further details, visit "OIG Compliance Program for Individual and Small Group Physician Practices" at

http://oig.hhs.gov/authorities/docs/physician. pdf

Computer System

Consider the following questions regarding computer systems:

- What software should be used for billing, for medical records, and for tracking quality data?

- Is your software compatible with Medicare and Medicaid systems?

- Is it suitable for fulfilling the federal standards for e-prescription?

- How many terminals are required?
- What are the procedures for entering medical record data?
- What type of networking is required?
- What types of Internet and email services are needed?
- What are the policies for patient confidentiality and privacy of data kept on a computer?

Compile Facts about Clients

Compile as many facts about the clients and practice as possible for use with other providers and insurers. These facts are also useful for marketing purposes.

Confidentiality

Your practice must have a HIPAA compliance plan. For more details, visit https://hipaatraining. net/compliance-template/ and

https://www.hipaatraining.net/HIPAA-Compliance-Template-Suites.pdf

Credentialing

The office manager should keep the following items for each NP:

- A copy of the current state license of the NP as an advanced practice nurse

- A copy of the current certification of the NP by a certifying authority

- A copy of at least two professional references, including their names, contact numbers, addresses, titles, nature of the professional relationship with an employee, and any recommendation related to the employee's clinical potential and working abilities with a team

- A statement of the malpractice history of the NP

- In many states, the NP must have a practice agreement in written form with the collaborating physician under which the NP is practicing

- NPs require DEA (Drug Enforcement Administration) numbers and may also need state CDS (controlled dangerous substance) numbers

- A copy of the current CPR (cardiopulmonary resuscitation) card of the NP

- The National Provider Identifier of the NP

Doctors

If your state requires physician collaboration, you may contract or hire a physician to deliver consulting services and sign a written agreement as per law. A physician may take an annual or monthly fee, a fixed rate per hour of consultation time, a small percentage of the income, or other negotiated arrangements that are agreeable between you and the physician. You may establish a partnership with a physician, in which liabilities and profits are shared among the partners.

Different Forms

Your organization should have all the relevant forms for these items:

- Patient intake (name, contact details, address, date of birth, insurance company and numbers, etc.)

- History and physical examination

- Care plan

- Tracking of healthcare maintenance and screening
- Referral form
- Progress note
- Appointment slips
- Return to work
- Appointments (calendar)
- Billing/encounter
- Release of PHI
- General consent form for treatment
- Consent form for specific procedures
- Patient instructions
- Lab report flow sheet
- Vital sign flow sheet
- Patient contact
- Notice of patient privacy rights

Durable Equipment

There are different durable medical equipment companies in every state. You can also search

....

on the web or through brokers for used medical equipment.

Emergency Plan

Always develop a written emergency plan that should cover the following areas:

- The level of emergency care from the NP
- The referral criteria for referring to the nearest emergency department
- The criteria for calling 911
- The criteria for ambulance transport
- Emergency plan for the patient loss of consciousness or other serious emergencies
- Plan for fire on the premises

Employees

Your organization should carry workers' compensation insurance, health insurance, and payroll insurance for employees as per state laws.

Equipment

There should be a refrigerator with ice-making facilities. Different medications should be placed in a separate refrigerator from specimens and staff lunches. Calibrate these refrigerators and all other necessary equipment at least annually.

Health Maintenance Organizations

Many HMOs (health maintenance organizations) contract with NP practices to become panel members. When the address and contact number of your practice are set, you can contact local HMOs about becoming a panel member.

Housekeeping

Housekeeping may cover the following aspects:

1. **Cleaning:** contract for a cleaning service to specify that how often cleaning is required and what should be done. It should be a minimum of three times a week.

2. **Extermination:** at least twice a month is reasonable.

3. **Snow removal:** businesses are often responsible for snow removal from the parking lot as well as the entranceway.

4. **Hazardous waste removal:** your practice should establish policies for hazardous waste

removal. Separate red bags should be placed in each examination room. On filling, the bags should be stored in a larger marked can or box. Waste disposal companies pick up hazardous waste at a monthly minimum rate.

Hazardous Wastes

The practice needs red plastic containers (marked as hazardous waste containers) for sharp instruments and needles as per law. These red containers then go in boxes supplied by a hazardous waste disposal company, which should be picked up monthly, at a minimum. Bloody materials and diapers should be deposited in red bags, which should be tied and placed into larger boxes. You must need waste disposal services for the disposal of hazardous wastes.

Information Sheets for Patients

Develop effective patient handouts, website references, tapes, and videos on a regular basis. Display the information material in offices, waiting rooms, or bathrooms.

....

Insurance

Your practices will require premises, payroll, professional liability, workers' compensation, and employee health insurance.

Laboratory Compliance

A laboratory, even if it only does pregnancy and urine dipstick tests, must be approved by the federal and state governments. You must obtain and fill out the paperwork required to comply with federal (CLIA) and state (State Laboratory Administration) requirements.

Laundry

You can use drapes and paper gowns. Linens can be laundered by an outside company. Laundries often need a fixed monthly minimum charge, which may be expensive for a newly established practice.

Library

Various books are indispensable, such as:

- Primary care handbook

- Drug facts and comparisons

- Skincare book with pictures

- Lab test reference book

- Guidelines to antibiotics therapy for the current year from the CDC

- STD (sexually transmitted disease) guidelines for the current year from the CDC

- The latest algorithm for healthcare screening and maintenance

Malpractice Insurance

Multiple different companies sell malpractice insurance to NPs. You can find promotions for these companies in any of the journals for NPs.

Marketing

Consider newspaper articles and ads regarding the opening of the practice. You may ask for TV coverage if your NP practice is a novel idea in your area. Also, check that the practice is listed in provider directories. Consider using social media and developing your website. Send email flyers, direct mail, or have someone distribute flyers in your local neighborhood. Announce your practice in NP publications, to your colleague NPs, and at NP meetings, and request for referrals. Also, inform local physicians about your practice and request referrals.

Nurses

Family NPs are the most common and beneficial class of NP for a small practice because they can handle all age groups. In terms of non-educational assets, compatibility, productivity, experience in primary care, flexibility, and resourcefulness are all necessary. Depending on patient requirements, your practice may offer the services of addiction counselors and nurse psychotherapists.

Operational Hours of Practice

Some MCOs (managed-care organizations) require that a practice maintain certain hours of operation as per state laws. Barring that requirement, your practice is free to establish your own hours.

On-Call Service

24-hour on-call service is a prerequisite from some insurers. You can use an answering machine that provides the beeper or telephone number of the individual on call. You may also use an answering service.

OSHA Compliance

The main requirements under the OSHA (Occupational Safety and Health Act) are to use personal protective equipment (PPEs) – gloves, masks, gowns, and goggles – when at risk while direct handling blood and other body fluid; the collection of hazardous waste materials; and the disposal of hazardous waste.

Private Insurers

Insurance companies often have a process for enlisting providers. You should develop a list of insurers' names, contact details, and addresses. The provider relations office of each company should be called to provide the following details:

- The company's policy regarding reimbursement for NP services

- The process for reimbursement
- The process through which an NP applies for a provider number

Patients

Think as well as plan for sources for new patients and ways to maintain established patients. Marketing and advertising are the best options.

Patients with Disabilities

Your practice should be wheelchair accessible to avoid unlawful discrimination for patients with disabilities.

Pharmaceuticals Stock

State regulations may control the authority of an NP to dispense medications. You may need a limited stock of commonly used medications. As for controlled substances, you have to follow the guidelines from the regulatory authorities.

Physical Space

Consider proper space for:

- Conference room
- Exam rooms
- Laboratory
- Play area for children
- Waiting area
- Utility room
- Offices
- Storage

Prescribing

In many states, NPs require separate licensure from the prescriptive authority. If NPs want to prescribe controlled substances, they will need a state CDS number and a DEA number. There is a fee for the state and DEA registration. NPs must follow state laws when prescribing or dispensing medications. You may consider the state board of nursing a good initial point for information about prescribing requirements.

Purchasing

Establish standing accounts with the following common companies: pharmacy, hazardous waste disposal, medical supply company, answering service, cleaning, telephone, medical equipment, printing, equipment repair, and office supplies.

Quality Assurance Plan

Develop a mission statement for your business and post it. Establish a method of assessment for staff and conduct regular self-evaluations. Adopt appropriate clinical practice guidelines and healthcare maintenance and screening guidelines. Do periodic chart reviews to evaluate that providers are following the practice's guidelines.

RNs, LPNs

If payment for encounters is not tied to MD or NPs, a practice may find that visits to LPNs or RNs can be beneficial to patients.

Referrals

Always keep a referral directory and update it on a regular basis. The referral directory may include names and contact numbers of referral sources for the following:

- Chest x-rays

- Counseling regarding unwanted pregnancy
- Cardiac assessment
- Dermatology assessment
- Dentistry
- Genetic counseling
- Drug and alcohol counseling
- HIV testing
- Gastrointestinal and genitourinary evaluation
- Head, eyes, ears, nose, and throat evaluation
- Mammograms
- Marriage or family counseling
- Neurologic assessment
- Orthopedic assessment
- Social work
- Psychiatric care
- Sexually transmitted infection screening
- Surgical assessment
- Protective services
- Counseling

Regulatory Matters

Every medical practice laboratory requires either frequent inspection by CLIA or a letter of exception demonstrating that an inspection is not needed. For more details, call the state health's laboratory division of the state department.

Reimbursement

Set up a patient intake process by which your practice can make sure that insurance information is up to date. For example, check the insurance card of the patient, get a copy of that card, and verify the information through a telephone number listed on the card. If the patient has no coverage, work out the payment process as per your practice policies.

Screening Patients for Medicaid Eligibility

The patient should be screened for Medicaid eligibility (screen the low-income patients with children and adults with disabilities).

Smartphones, Computers, Fax, and Copying Machines

Your practice should have at least one of each. However, you should follow HIPAA guidelines to protect the patient's privacy and confidentiality.

Storage

Vaccines must be stored in a refrigerator, with a thermostat keeping them at the required temperature. Other non-controlled substances should be placed out of public display. Controlled substances should be kept in double-locked storage. Maintain the records of the dispensing and on-hand supply of each dose.

Security

Most may also need a security guard, depending on drafting a strategy about after-hours use of the office by staff members. Establish a policy for cash handling collected during the day and do not keep large sums of cash in the office.

Standard of Care

You should consult the latest journals, books, and attend at least one conference per year to know the guidelines regarding the modern standard of care.

Start-Up Funding

Develop a business plan and take the plan to a bank for a business loan. If rejected, you can apply to the local Small Business Administration for a loan.

Stationery

Your practice will need business cards, letterhead and envelopes, prescription cards, appointment cards, patient education brochures, and promotional brochures.

Support Staff

The support staff may include a receptionist, billing manager, lab technician, marketing specialist, housekeeper, and handyman.

Written Agreement

In many states, NPs need a written and signed collaborative agreement with a physician to specify their scope of practice.

References

1. Boyle, P. (2021, June 11). *Aging patients and doctors drive nation's physician shortage*. AAMC. https://www.aamc.org/news-insights/aging-patients-and-doctors-drive-nation-s-physician-shortage

2. Neergård, G. (2020). Entrepreneurial nurses in the literature: A systematic literature review. *Journal of Nursing Management, 29*(5), 905–915. https://doi.org/10.1111/jonm.13210.

3. Wojciechowski, M. (2021, April 29). *Nurse Practitioners: Opening Your Own Practice*. Minority Nurse. https://minoritynurse.com/nurse-practitioners-opening-your-own-practice/.

4. Kershaw, B. (2011). The Future of Nursing – Leading Change, Advancing

Health the Future of Nursing – Leading Change, Advancing Health. *Nursing Standard, 26*(7), 31. https://doi.org/10.7748/ns2011.10.26.7.31.b1274

5.   Chou, C. F. & lo Sasso, A. T. (2009). Practice Location Choice by New Physicians: The Importance of Malpractice Premiums, Damage Caps, and Health Professional Shortage Area Designation. *Health Services Research, 44*(4), 1271–1289. https://doi.org/10.1111/j.1475-6773.2009.00976.x.

6.   Walczak, J. & Cammenga, J. (2021b, December 15). *2021 State Business Tax Climate Index*. Tax Foundation. https://taxfoundation.org/2021-state-business-tax-climate-index/.

7.   *How does passion drive sales?* (2020, November 2). Profit.Co. https://www.profit.co/blog/the-alphabet-p/passion/how-does-passion-drive-sales/.

8.   De Vore, S. (2019, September 10). *Why Passion is Essential to Entrepreneurship and Building a Thriving Business.*

. . . .

Youpreneur.Com - How to Build, Market and Monetize Your Personal Brand! https://youpreneur.com/why-passion-is-essential-to-entrepreneurship-and-building-a-thriving-business/.

9.   Juda, E. (2021, June 3). *Where Can Nurse Practitioners Work Without Physician Supervision? | Simmons Online*. SC-UMT. https://online.simmons.edu/blog/nurse-practitioners-scope-of-practice-map/.

10.   American Nurse Today. (2021, January 27). *NP role in medication-assisted treatment for opioid use disorder*. American Nurse. https://www.myamericannurse.com/np-medication-treatment-opioid-disorder/.

11.   Writers, S. (2021, October 22). *Meet a Cosmetic Nurse | Nursejournal.org*. NurseJournal. https://nursejournal.org/articles/meet-a-cosmetic-nurse/.

12.   Sam. (2021, February 15). *5 Steps to Becoming an Aesthetic Nurse Practitioner*. The American Association of Aesthetic Medicine and Surgery

. . . .

(AAAMS). https://aaams.net/
articles/5-steps-to-becoming-an-
aesthetic-nurse-practitioner/.

13. International Association for Physicians in
    Aesthetic Medicine. (2021b, October 5).
    Medical Aesthetic Nurse Practitioners.
    IAPAM. https://iapam.com/training/
    medical-aesthetic-nurse-practitioners.

14. J. (2021, April 6). *Why You Should
    Consider Opening a Medical
    Weight Loss Clinic*. The Elite Nurse
    Practitioner. https://elitenp.com/
    why-you-should-consider-opening-
    a-medical-weight-loss-clinic/.

15. NursePreneurs. (2021, December
    6). *IV Hydration Course – Top
    NursePreneurs | NursePreneurs*.
    NursePreneurs | Changing Healthcare
    One Nurse Business at A Time. https://
    nursepreneurs.com/ivhydration/.

16. Kelman, M. (2019, December 6).
    *Development and implementation
    of a nurse-led allergy clinic model in
    primary care: feasibility trial protocol*.

. . . .

Nature. https://www.nature.com/articles/s41533-019-0155-5.

17. Chlan, L. L., Tofthagen, C., & Terzic, A. (2019). The Regenerative Horizon: Opportunities for Nursing Research and Practice. *Journal of Nursing Scholarship*, *51*(6), 651–660. https://doi.org/10.1111/jnu.12520.

18. Balestra, M. (2018). Telehealth and Legal Implications for Nurse Practitioners. *The Journal for Nurse Practitioners*, *14*(1), 33–39. https://doi.org/10.1016/j.nurpra.2017.10.003.

19. Whelchel, M. (2021, March 5). *How to start an NP telemedicine business*. NPHub. https://nphub.com/blog/np-telemedicine-business-guide/.

20. Klein, T. A. & Bindler, R. (2021). Ask Your Provider About Cannabis: Increasing Nurse Practitioner Knowledge and Confidence. *Cannabis and Cannabinoid Research*. Published. https://doi.org/10.1089/can.2021.0061.

21. Garde, D. (2018, October 10). *As ketamine clinics spread, so do start-your-own-business courses*. STAT. https://www.statnews.com/2018/10/11/ketamine-clinics-training-courses-pop-up/.

22. American Medical Association. (2019, July 19). *A strong advising team can help your private practice flourish*. https://www.ama-assn.org/practice-management/private-practices/strong-advising-team-can-help-your-private-practice-flourish.

23. Writers, S. (2021b, December 13). *How to Become a Nurse Practitioner | NurseJournal.org*. NurseJournal. https://nursejournal.org/nurse-practitioner/how-to-become-a-np/.

24. Jain, H. (2021, July 5). *How to Improve Patient Flow in Clinics*. LeadSquared. https://www.leadsquared.com/how-to-improve-patient-flow-in-clinics/.

25. Notte, C., & Skolnik, N. (2010). Choosing the Right EHR for Your Practice. *Family Practice News, 40*(2), 58. https://doi.org/10.1016/s0300-7073(10)70160-2.

. . . .

26. Sastow, G. E. S. (2016, February 19). *Choosing a Business Entity for Your Medical Practice*. Oncology Practice Management. https://uropracticemanagement.com/issues/2016-02-19-14-52-47/june-2016-vol-5-no-3/2778-choosing-a-business-entity-for-your-medical-practice.

27. Rutledge, C. & Gustin, T. (2021). Preparing Nurses for Roles in Telehealth: Now is the Time! *OJIN: The Online Journal of Issues in Nursing, 26*(1). https://doi.org/10.3912/ojin.vol26no01man03.

28. *Telehealth for Family Nurse Practitioners: Virtual Healthcare*. (2021, November 11). Marymount University Online. https://online.marymount.edu/blog/telehealth-for-family-nurse-practitioners.

29. Resnick, B. & Nettina, S. (2010). Should a Written Collaborative Practice Agreement with a Physician Be Required for Nurse Practitioner Practice? *The Journal for Nurse Practitioners, 6*(3), 199–200. https://doi.org/10.1016/j.nurpra.2010.02.002.

. . . .

30. Brunner, S. (2019, February 26). *Physicians Benefit from Collaboration with NPs and PAs*. MedSource Consultants. https://medsourceconsultants. com/physicians-benefit-from- collaboration-with-nps-and-pas/.

31. Gandolf, S. (2020, August 12). *Healthcare Marketing: 15 Strategies to Gain More Patients | Healthcare Success, the Healthcare Marketing Agency*. Healthcare Success. https:// healthcaresuccess.com/blog/ healthcare-marketing/healthcare- marketing-strategy.html.

32. Duquesne University. (2020, October 26). *Nurse Practitioners Turned Entrepreneurs: How NPs are changing the World*. Duquesne University School of Nursing. https:// onlinenursing.duq.edu/blog/nurse- practitioners-turned-entrepreneurs- how-nps-are-changing-the-world/.

33. Phillips, C. N. B. P. (2015, October 15). *Social Media for NPs*. Nurse

Practitioners in Business. https://npbusiness.org/socialmedia/.

34. American Association of Nurse Practitioners. (2019, March 8). *How to Market Your NP Practice.* https://www.aanp.org/news-feed/how-to-market-your-practice.

More books by
Dr. Scharmaine Lawson

Fiction

- Nola The Nurse®, She's On The Go Series Vol 1 (available in Spanish and French)

- Nola The Nurse® & Friends Explore The Holi Fest, She's On The Go Series Vol 2

- Nola The Nurse® & Friends Explore The Holi Fest, She's On The Go Series Vol 2 coloring book

- Nola The Nurse® & Bax Join The Protest

- Nola the Nurse & Bax Join The Protest coloring book

- Nola The Nurse® Activity Book for Preschool Vol 1

- Nola The Nurse® Activity Book for Kindergarten Vol 2

- Nola The Nurse® Math Worksheets for Kindergarten Vol 3

- Nola The Nurse® English/Sight Worksheets for Kindergarten Vol 4

- Nola The Nurse® Math/English Worksheets for Preschoolers Vol 5

- Nola The Nurse® Math Worksheets for First Graders Vol 6

- Nola The Nurse® STEM Activity Book for 5–8-year-olds Vol 7

- Nola The Nurse® & Friends Explore The Holi Fest She's On The Go Series Vol 2

- Nola The Nurse® & Friends Explore The Holi Fest She's On The Go Series Vol 2 Coloring Book

- Nola The Nurse® Remembers Hurricane Katrina Special Edition

- Nola The Nurse® Remembers Hurricane Katrina Special Edition Coloring Book

- Nola The Nurse®: Let's Talk About Germs, The Germy series, Vol. 1

. . . .

- Nola The Nurse®: Let's Talk About Germs, The Germy series, Vol. 1 coloring book

- Nola The Nurse® How To Stop Those Yuck Germs, The Germy series, Vol 2

- Nola The Nurse® How To Stop Those Yuck Germs, The Germy series, Vol 2 coloring book

- Nola The Nurse® & her Super Friends Learn About Mardi Gras Safety, Holiday series, Vol 1

- Nola The Nurse® & her Super Friends Learn About Mardi Gras Safety, Holiday series, Vol 1 coloring book

- Nola The Nurse® Cursive Handwriting Workbook For Kids

- Nola The Nurse® Science Word & Puzzle Search For Kids

- Nola The Nurse® Mandala Coloring Book for kids

- Nola The Nurse® Coloring Book for Kids

- Black Dot

....

Non-Fiction

- Housecalls 101: The only book you will ever need to begin your medical practice, Part I

- Housecalls 101: A Clinician's Guide To In-Home Health Care, Telemedicine Services, and Long-Distance Treatment For a Post-Pandemic World, Part II

- Housecalls 101 Policy & Procedure Manual

- Culture Stories: Racism, Bias, and Prejudice in Nursing (soon to be released)

- Pandemic Parenting

- The Business of Nur$ing: The Blueprint

⊕ www.NolaTheNurse.com

⊕ www.DrLawsonNP.com

 **Podcast**

Nite Nite Nurse Podcast

⊕ https://open.spotify.com/show/3nGnfpXTUfVUx2mQTrsWr G?si=1881e7a2728545fe

⊕ DrLawson@DrLawsonNP.com

. . . .

CPSIA information can be obtained
at www.ICGtesting.com
Printed in the USA
BVHW031055300323
661447BV00012B/712